+13.95

The Pits and the Pendulum

of related interest

Freaks, Geeks and Asperger Syndrome
A User Guide to Adolescence
Luke Jackson
ISBN 1 84310 098 3

Pretending to be Normal
Living with Asperger's Syndrome
Liane Holliday Willey
ISBN 1 85302 749 9

Cracked
Recovering After Traumatic Brain Injury
Lynsey Calderwood
ISBN 1 84310 065 7

The Pits and the Pendulum

A Life with Bipolar Disorder

Brian Adams

Jessica Kingsley Publishers
London and Philadelphia

First published in the United Kingdom in 2003
by Jessica Kingsley Publishers Ltd
116 Pentonville Road
London N1 9JB, England
and
325 Chestnut Street
Philadelphia, PA 19106, USA
www.jkp.com

Copyright © 2003 Brian Adams

Library of Congress Cataloging in Publication Data
Adams, Brian, 1946-
   The pits and the pendulum : a life with bipolar / Brian Adams.
   p.cm.
   ISBN 1-84310-104-1 (pbk. : alk paper)
   1. Adams, Brian, 1946- 2. manic-depressive illness--Patients--Great Britain--Biography.
   I. Title.

RC516 A32 2002
616.89'5'0092--dc21
[B]   2002070915

British Library Cataloguing in Publication Data
A CIP catalogue record for this book is available from the British Library

ISBN 1 84310 104 1

Printed and Bound in Great Britain by
Athenaeum Press, Gateshead, Tyne and Wear

Contents

Winston Churchill, Pablo Picasso, Christopher Columbus, Lord Byron, David Livingstone, Tony Hancock, Abraham Lincoln, Edgar Allan Poe, Robert Burns, Alexander the Great, Spike Milligan, Vivien Leigh, Napoleon, Mao Tse-tung…and *Me.*

Not a Survivor's Guide

I wondered about how to tackle a book about my manic depression for some time. In January 1998 I saw how and this is the result.

Sometimes when I wrote I was a bit down, sometimes I was high and sometimes I was even higher up than that and so different versions of me have contributed to this book. The writing, therefore, reflects this, containing different shades and moods, not to mention the contradictions. But that is all right for it is illustrative of the illness itself and whilst I believe that the little factual information I give on the illness is accurate, this book is not a survivor's guide or anything of the sort. It is just a tour of manic depression which I hope will communicate something of the character of the illness to non-sufferers and strike some chords with my fellow manic-depressives. It is also written for my family and friends who until they read the first draft were only able to see the effects of the illness. I also wrote the book for myself.

My thanks to the following for their encouragement and help in the production of this book: Fiona Moncrieff, Kelvin Paisley, Christine and John Ritchie, Carole Sands, Dr Douglas Fowlie, Bob Watson, Mike Harley, Marion Newton, Alasdair Macrone and Hilary Winter.

Glasgow Dawn

The fourth floor attic I shared with Ian in February 1970 had just a few months previously been occupied by a Glasgow criminal. Curious, the upgrading that 'criminal' gets when attached to 'Glasgow'. An Aberdeen criminal could be a horse-thief for all that means but the prefix 'Glasgow' surely means that your man is a killer, as indeed this Glaswegian was. After a shoot-out from our flat and a chase across the city he was shot and killed by police.

Ian, my flatmate, and I were community education students at Jordanhill College of Education and on viewing the flat had been far more impressed with the cheap rent than the flat's notoriety. The landlady told us all about the previous tenant. She had been suspicious of him from the start: 'He put in that new door lock on his first day!' We gasped politely at the lock, paid a week's rent in advance and moved into this tiny piece of Glasgow's history.

At four o'clock on this particular morning I was not thinking about late members of the criminal underworld. Rather, I was thinking about my own world and of how it had been disrupted by the thing that was going to keep me working until another city dawn. I was writing my final thesis on the subject of group dynamics but putting far more work into the project than was necessary. It had become an obsession. If there were any more books to read on the subject, the college and the rest of the city's libraries did not know about them as I consumed the bibliography like an athlete consumes air. Now the books lay piled amongst my notes, my fags and the rest of the swot's paraphernalia as I examined, compared and criticized the theory in the light of my practical experience.

I was already far beyond the number of words required by my tutor but I cared not. Everything that occurred to me in my elated state seemed crucially important and, feeling at times more observer than author, I watched my ideas and observations flood on to the lined foolscap pads in a joyful long-hand stream.

Ian, my flatmate, lay asleep only a yard from the kitchen table where I worked by the light of a small cheap lamp. He could sleep through a hurricane and had proved it a few years before when he woke to find half of Glasgow wrecked by one. My coffee-making trips to the sink and gas ring that were our kitchen were not going to disturb him.

He was a good bloke, Ian, just as tolerant of me when he was awake which was just as well. All I could talk to him about when our paths crossed (he diurnal, me nocturnal) was my latest vital insight into *The Group* – his day and how the rest of the world was doing was of no interest whatsoever to me.

I did not feel ridiculous or selfish or irresponsible. My only concern was an occasional vague feeling of unease at being unable to work on my thesis and carry on with the rest of my life as well. This new thing puzzled me but it would have made no difference to know what it was.

Something fundamental had happened; over for good were the days when I would rise bright-eyed to attend lectures then, after a bit of work in the library, take off with Ian and my other college friends for a pint and a pie. Nothing mattered now but my work and the important truths I knew it contained. The light shadows of doubt that made me pause were short-lived; there was this idea to perfect and then I would go to bed and really try to attend morning lectures.

But going to bed soon would never happen, there was always something that had to be gone over just one more time.

I was in my early twenties and life had taken a remarkable turn. From the bakehouse in Aberdeen, Scotland where I had served my apprenticeship I had entered a world which until recently had only shown itself in the varsity-scarfed and duffel-coated students I used to view from the tops of corporation buses. At school I had never achieved a thing and although I had done well enough to win a place on the college course, my academic mediocrity continued here where there was hardly an exam I did not just scrape through despite being fascinated by most of the subjects.

I do not think I was stupid or lazy. Looking back on the time, fear of exams and poor concentration were the problems. A swot I was not but, hey, it was the sixties; I was idealistic, energetic, had some natural gifts, was not frightened to speak up and although exams did stress me, I had never been asked by my tutors to do better. So what was all this sudden application to things difficult and academic? This was obsession with a capital 'M'. I believe that this was my first experience of mania.

A few weeks after handing in the thesis I found myself confused when I sank into being the opposite of what I had been throughout the college course. I could not get out of bed and an emptiness seemed to have invaded everything. I felt unhappy and isolated, started to think about God and death a lot and would weep for hours at some of the miserable thoughts I was having. In this condition the effort required to show up for the few lectures I did attend was immense and I also became socially unreliable. This, I am sure, was my first experience of depression.

I had not even heard of depression as an illness and certainly had never heard of manic depression; a manic-depressive, though, is what I had become.

I completed the course without anybody having spotted that I was ill, as indeed neither had I. On the Isle of Arran on the west coast of Scotland I spent an idyllic sunny summer as warden of a Scottish youth hostel; then, refreshed, moved over to the east coast to begin my first professional post as a youth leader in Fife.

The thesis? When our efforts were returned to us I could not understand the marking on mine and had to ask Ian what 'A+' meant. It was an 'A plus' – excellence with knobs on! This is where the plot is supposed to say I got an 'F'. What kind of illness is this?

1

Legoland and Holes in the Head – Mania

Manic depression can simply be described as a psychiatric illness which causes extreme swings in mood. In mania there are periods of elation, excitement and sometimes delusions combined with loss of judgement and inhibitions. This can result in a rapid flow of ideas, often imaginative, but it can also progress to a loss of a sense of reality. At other times, depression occurs which can be prolonged and overwhelming. The illness can be of the kind in which only depressions occur or one in which both 'high' and 'low' swings are experienced. Some people are rapid swingers, i.e. four or more complete mood cycles in a year. Some can complete a mood cycle in days, even in hours, and a mixed state can be experienced in which both manic and depressive episodes are experienced. The term 'bipolar mood disorder' is also used to describe the illness.

I do not know if I am unusual or not, but in my manic-depressive career I have experienced nearly all of the above as the illness turns, ducks and dives eluding my attempts to get to grips with it. Manic depression, though, is not a virus or a parasite, it is my own chemistry that tyrannizes me – manic depression is thought to be almost certainly genetic in origin. I have never thought that there was a cure for my manic depression. I attempt to understand it, of course, and try to learn to live with it but never really have.

In its milder forms the state is called hypomania but I find it more helpful to measure my condition on a scale of one to ten. A 'one' is hardly noticeable: unaccountably feeling good and confident, a bit restless. Nothing unusual about that; everybody I know experiences this from time to time, but multiply that enjoyable state by five and stay that way for too long and you have a problem. If a 'ten' is completely crackers then I reckon I have been up there a few times in deep trouble with an 'eight'. What I first experienced as a student would have been hypomania – a 'three' or 'four'.

That first high was a state of being I have lived through many times since and is one which I experience now with a rising 'four' as I write this chapter. This is a state in which I am driven into obsessional, intense periods of creativity in which I am able to pour enormous amounts of energy into whatever activity I have become focused upon. These events come without warning and the activity itself is completely unpredictable. It can be physical and useful, as in the times I have moved mountains in garden landscaping, or it can power me up to write a play in a week – for which I won a £700 prize in a national playwrighting competition. There was also my 'A plus' thesis: highly useful academically, but disabling too in that it was socially disastrous.

At other times, the end product of this manic energy can be utterly meaningless and trivial. I once lost a week obsessed by Lego. Day after day I would explore the possibilities of the medium, trying this little house in that colour, a spaceship in these stripes. Sometimes I would just stack the pieces up in long columns with the colours ordered in intensely pleasing layers or lay them out in flat symmetrical patterns. Somehow the bright primary colours seemed to speak to me, demanding that I explore their potential along with the rest of Lego's fascinating possibilities. Lego, I was sure, was what I was meant to be, what I was created for. I'll get a job with Lego now and build Lego houses and Lego spaceships for a living. With my talent for Lego I'll make a fortune. I'll get a letter off to Lego today to tell them all about me. I need to buy more Lego. Which I did, boxes of it. I am still too embarrassed to say how much time and money I spent on bloody Lego.

A new situation for me at this time was that during this full-time obsession I was also a full-time freelance journalist and living happily with a woman I loved and her three children whom I also loved. From the secret place I had made into Legoland I would return home knackered after a hard day at the Legoface.

'Hi, Honey, I'm home.'

The sofa after tea was its usual gerbil's nest of kids and me as they cuddled up with their patter and news from school and playgroup, but I was thinking about Lego. 'Let's go play with the Lego,' I would say; but they were sick of it, wanted to play cards instead.

At a certain point in the Lego business I got sick of it too, as always happens in the daft highs when it starts to become uncomfortable and I realize what has happened to me again. But dawning insight does not free me from the obsession. The obsession will only go in its own time and there is nothing I can do to rid myself of it.

Except for drugs, that is. I could go and get some from the doctor but they turn me into something else that is also unacceptable; some of them are cosh therapy – like a blow to the head they put an end to everything.

A doctor able to enter your psychosis would be much more fun:

Doc What seems to be the trouble?

Me Lego.

Doc Yes, there's quite a bit of it going about. You keep running out of doors, right?

Me All the time.

Doc   [*Reaching for his prescription pad.*] That's a bugger, I'll write you up a month's supply. How are you off for windows?

An obsession with the card game Solitaire is another ridiculous example as was the time of the 'Poisonous Coos': plastic toy cows I painted in bright, gaudy colours to advertize to predators that they were poisonous. But was it art? Of course it was. I planned a one-man exhibition that would also include my plastic herd of yellow and black checked sheep. Their colour and pattern would allow them to graze safely at airfields. Get it? The sheep would be easy to spot by pilots when they strayed on to the runway. I would set up dioramas of livestock sales in which the humans were in the pens with the animals doing the buying. In the animal research/old jokes feature there would be lots of sick combinations: sheep/kangaroo crosses (for woolly jumpers) and four-legged chickens – 'I hear they've developed four-legged chickens but they don't know what they taste like yet.' 'Why not?' 'They can't catch them!'

Sadly, I found an art teacher who wanted to work with me in a joint exhibition.

There was the Mull high when at the end of an arduous week-long trek in the mountains I could not stop speaking to anyone with whom I made eye contact, which on that glorious summer's morning was the queue at Craignure waiting for the Oban ferry. The entertainment included my removing a walking stick from a hirpling Geordie.

Manic-depressive
        That's a fine stick.

Geordie   Aye, I twisted me ankle yesterdea.

Manic-depressive
        Mmnnn, but is it a good balancer. Let's see.

[Manic-depressive takes the stick and balances it expertly on a foot then on to his nose – as this one can.]

Then there was the byre high when for five long days I could not stop cleaning and reorganizing my byre. Where pigs and milk cows once lived it up, after I had finished you could have conducted open-heart surgery. Every rusted shard of nail that had desecrated its stone walls and roof timbers over the century had to be extracted and every last strand of cobweb sucked out in the spider equivalent of some appalling natural disaster. Old bulbous meat paste jars, desiccated sparrows and vile, collapsed DDT packets still with their soup-spoon measures were extracted from cavities which until then were only known to the mice. I even found an early Lego piece. It left me cold though – I had moved on to perfect byres.

I had used that byre as a workshop for nine contented years without ever thinking in that time that the place needed a special doing, but suddenly, all this, the pursuit of perfection, had to be followed to the exclusion of everything else in my life.

The perfection theme gets carried quite frequently into every cupboard and drawer in the house – the need for and the location of every item is reassessed. The order created is intensely pleasing with repeated visits made to the sites to view the results once more and, as was the case with the byre episode, it will not necessarily end when I go to bed; in half an hour I will be up and looking at my work again and, in my pyjamas, be putting in another hour on some crucial detail missed.

When a high has passed I look to see what harm has been done. Manic mucking out of byres and showing off to ferry queues and other such episodes is now something I have learned to let pass with a shake of the head. Where, however, some serious indiscretion has been committed the reckoning can be considerable. Several times in 'après-mania' I have come out in a cold sweat when I have realized what I have done. Some of these were feats of law breaking the details of which wild horses are not going to drag out of me here except to say that they were out and out acts of theft and vandalism. At the time they seemed justified and funny, even important, but they would have had terrible consequences for me if I had been caught.

Financial disaster awaits the manic-depressive and his family when he sees himself as a budding Bill Gates. Three times I have started up in self-employment and lost thousands as a consequence and maybe lost as much again on various notions and enthusiasms which would not let me sleep until I was clearing out my savings again. I hear that wise manic-depressives have their financial affairs put into a trust. If I had known back then what the problem was maybe I might have gone for that option but on yet another certain route to fame and fortune, although the evidence of previous follies was all around staring me in the face and screaming in my ears, it never seemed that there was anything wrong. When this book hits the best-selling list, first thing, I will set up a trust to stand between my millions and me.

But first there is this high I am experiencing right now to deal with. After as black a depression as any I have experienced I suddenly found I had to write. It started with a long letter to a friend, followed by a chapter of this book.

It has sunk in now what has happened again and I know, after twenty-seven years of it, what is to come but, as ever, insight makes no difference. It is now 2.21am and I started work at 7.30am (nineteen hours ago) after just four hours sleep. Yesterday I tried to distract myself for a bit by watching a bit of favourite television. I could not enjoy it though, could not even sit down to view it and watched it hopping about from behind a chair – my mind upstairs in the study, all the time thinking of the writing.

Tonight I should have been practising with my musical partner for a gig we have tomorrow but, using the small snowdrifts along my track as an excuse, I cancelled it. If a gas leak blew up the old folk's home we are to perform in, I would see the positive side. The fire in the living room downstairs has not been lit in a week as I have given up trying to be anywhere but here in my study. I will try to finish at 3am but I know right now that I will not; always there is that final paragraph to do a little more work on to keep me at it for another two hours. It has started now to become very unpleasant, no longer the joy of the first writings. I would like to sit down to a bit of telly, maybe go for a walk, take the gun and come back with a rabbit to casserole but that is not possible. I can only leave this room for peanut butter sandwiches, tea and the toilet.

The stuff comes out easily enough; it is the obsessional revising that is so uncomfortable. But asking the doc for something to slow me down is unthinkable. Not just because the medication is unpleasant but because yesterday I was the slob version of me, today I'm this one: productive, alive and optimistic. I'll take the pain, I don't care how manic I get; taking a drug to this would be an act of murder. This is surely crucial stuff. This book when published (I wonder who will do the Foreword) will offer a unique insight into the world of the manic-depressive and be required reading for all in the psychiatric field. With the right marketing best-selling status is certain. I will be invited on to TV chat shows where I will shine. Channel 4 and the BBC will look again at the playscripts they returned. A lecture tour will bring in another thirty thou… Get the picture? On the fantasies roll.

With dawning insight, though, another me can just be heard away in the distance, laughing in the background at my nonsense, telling me to get a grip. Eventually that voice will get through and the fantasies will fade away to be filed under 'Highs-Past'.

No telling of famous highs is complete without the hole-in-the-head high, which took place at an isolated cottage where I once lived. I had become obsessed by the building of things – largish joinery projects utilizing a pile of scrap wood I had acquired. Typically, everything had to be started and finished in one go and, stopping for only a few hours' sleep in days and nights of manic activity, they were. I had finished a superb thirty-bird hen house and now moved on to making a dovecote.

A big enough thing it was: ten feet high, seven feet long and six feet wide. At a point close to completion I needed to use a sledge-hammer. Without going into the details of how such a thing is possible, I gave myself the most helluva clout on the head with it. Holding my head in my hands (as you do) I walked some distance up the track before wondering why, then backtracked to the house for a rake through my sawdust and blood-matted hair to see what damage had been done. Dirling* a lot and bleeding a dramatic red streak or two I did the right thing which was to get back to finishing the dovecote!

Maybe two hours on, with darkness, headache and nausea creeping up on me, the project was more or less complete despite the loss of more manic minutes when one of the dovecote doors crashed down upon that already sorely insulted head! Although elated and detached from everything but the wonderful, warm fantasies concerning my achievements to come in the pigeon fancy, at that point I do remember starting to feel a bit sorry for myself.

Filthy and ill I went to bed. I survived the manic attack: the dovecote got stocked with pigeons; the swelling went down in my head; the cut healed and the hole appeared in my skull.

---

*   Throbbing: a knock or blow causes the person or thing to 'dirl'.

Down the pub

Me   Hey, guys feel the hole in my head.

The Guys   [*Pushing their fingers a centimetre into my skull.*]
              Jesus!

Our diagnosis was a depressed fracture, which an x-ray confirmed. My doctor of that time said that I had been lucky, nature had healed things up. But it was worth going along just to see his reaction – for once he seemed interested in something I had brought him. 'Goodness,' he cussed, 'why didn't you seek medical attention?' 'And not finish the dovecote?' I did not explain.

Here then, in manic depression, is an illness which can brain you, earn top marks for academic dissertations, write award-winning plays, bankrupt you, get you a year for your first offence and, until such times as an 'A plus' in Lego brings a social or career leg-up, get you committed.

But cracks on the head are the least of the dangers. The flip-side of all of this is depression. People die from depression all the time. Many times, sometimes all of the time, I have wondered if it was going to get me.

2

The Pits – Depression

In manic-depressive imagery the pendulum is often utilized. For example, *Pendulum* is the title of the journal of the (English) Manic Depression Fellowship and, of course, 'pendulum' apprears in the title of this book. Yet, I have to say that the image of the pendulum has never really represented the chaotic nature of my manic depression and I wonder if there *are* sufferers out there who have a form of the illness which follows the predictable, placid swing of the pendulum.

But we must not take these things too seriously. We can see what they are getting at with '*Pendulum*'. What matters about the English mag is that it is a important publication for people like myself. I have to say though that *On the Level*, the newsletter of the Scottish Fellowship, is hopelessly optimistic but it does have the virtue of meaning something of an opposite to the English title.

What title would my rag have? I surely cannot be the first to have extracted 'MaD' from manic depression and although *MaD Monthly* or *MaDMAG* would make for a wonderfully confident and confrontational response to public attitudes towards mental illness, I concede that, at this time, I might be alone in rooting for it. *Time Bomb* occurs, but some joyful PMT support group will be off with that title. *In The Mood* is the newsletter of the Manic Depression Fellowship Aberdeen – good for them.

Roller Coaster appeals. Certainly the erratic ups and downs, twists and turns of a fairground ride is a far better metaphor for the manic depression I know. But even this falls short of perfect. Roller coasters are for kicks and, in my case, depression is the primary experience.

Nobody would pay to go on the rides in the manic-depressive theme park. Here, they all have a very unattractive feature: the bit when the cars draw you down and out of the colour and the laughter and the music to stop underground for an eternal minute – the fun of the fair a distant memory if remembered at all.

The tunnel, a common image amongst depression sufferers, is a place in which I am overwhelmed in a despair that invades everything of me. Here I cannot even weep. There is no more miserable place to be – this is 'The Pits' where there is only negativity, confusion, self-absorption and self-pity.

When I can put on a smile, wash my face or even start to see the joke, it does not mean that I am out of the tunnel or even that I can see light at the end of it, it just means that I am on my feet. 'Walking Wounded' was a description I read somewhere for this state.

Despite the appalling time I had with the illness in my mid-twenties and the harassment it gave me throughout my thirties and forties, the illness never completely got me down. A depression would lift or I would get out of another mania-led scrape and look around to see what was new. Always there was some new challenge waiting for me to take up and life would get back to being the sweet thing it had been before it had been spoiled. During these twenty-odd years I enjoyed every job I had, never felt pressured or was troubled by any career ambitions, was never driven by money or status and in my social life there was not a moment spent with people whose company I did not enjoy. And I was aware of this good life – many times I stopped consciously to congratulate myself on my good luck.

The choices on approaching my mid-fifties, on a low, fixed income and with this mental health record, are much reduced. The security and independence I have in the few comfortable bits and pieces I have gathered around me are too precious to risk on something that worked every time as a gallivanting twenty/thirty-something. Try any of that stuff now and I risk hostel beds and cardboard-lined shop doorways.

When life was sweeter I was never in any doubt as to when a depression had moved in but self-diagnosis is more difficult now. Very often what I have experienced in the last few years is, I am sure, a mixture of depression and plain unhappiness – my not yet having come to terms with relative poverty and the loss of a work challenge. The doctors have nothing in their bags for this. I'm working on a cure for my depressions though, starting with a big lottery win.

What, no more depressions after becoming a millionaire? A nice thought. I might have traded in the NHS for the private clinic in Geneva but mood swings have come out of the blue far too often for me to expect that a wealthy lifestyle is the key to staying on the level.

Assuming my millionaire lifestyle had not created a new set of difficulties, would my depressions be back to the easily recognizable form I fancy they took in my youth? I fear not. My head has taken too many hidings for things to be that straightforward any more. For as much as I was able to rise above my illness in my twenties and thirties, I am sure that the serial failures, hurts and scrapes were layering down and starting to muddy the emotional waters even then. How many times have I launched myself out on the hopeless mind-bashing quest for answers – an exercise which is probably, in itself, part of the depression process? How different, more complex, more messy a version of manic depression has crept into me now?

In The Pits I will relive and endlessly churn over every unpleasant thing I believe I did in my life, wrestling with insignificant incidents which everybody has long since forgotten but which still consume me in agonies of regret. I shout at the walls in an attempt to rid myself of the sounds and images which drown me in ten times the embarrassment and guilt they did when they first took place. Then there are the sins which have been perpetrated against me. The faces of the sinners fading in and out of my consciousness as the injustices against me play again and I plan retributions that make Charles Manson look like Sooty.

And what if these depressions, the bipolar me, are actually the symptom of something else altogether? Could this illness be self-inflicted; a hidey-hole where personalities like mine can escape from past hurts? Is this just a way of avoiding life's give and take? And look at the prescription drugs I take; to what extent is my thinking influenced by that daily cocktail? I hit a dog's breakfast of possibilities when I try to identify and understand the interplay of forces that inhabit my head.

This neurotic rake through your head for new ideas and new angles on your latest depression is, I am sure, a trap but another is to start seeing everything in yourself in terms of psychiatric illnesses: I feel good so I must be slightly manic; I feel a bit unwell so I must be depressed; I pigged out at the weekend so I've got an eating disorder; I could kill that bastard so I'm Hannibal Lecter.

Inflicting this junk upon yourself is bad enough but when others put in their tuppence worth another element is added to your guilt and confusion. Friends will tell you that there is nothing wrong with you or tell you exactly where you went wrong and what you should be doing to get a grip.

'I get pretty down myself sometimes, y'know.'

'We all have our ups and downs but we just have to get on with it.'

Understandably, people get tired of the depressive's self-absorption: I took these classics from friends I had valued for many years. I never called on them again – ignored their notes and Christmas cards. I will miss them forever but they were not safe places for me any more.

What though is depressed and what is unhappiness? Well, paralysis, for example, is not caused by being unhappy. In a shopping mall once a security man came up to me and asked if everything was all right. Only then did I realize that for some time I had been frozen to the same spot amongst the passing Christmas crowds. I had been depressed for some time and here I had drifted into 'zombie' while trying to decide what to do next with myself. The options tumbled over and over in my brain: go to the supermarket, the indoor market, the music shop – go home, then nothing. I have no idea how long I had been standing there but it was long enough for somebody to notice that something was wrong and say so – a first.

Early that morning, drawing on previous experience, I had hoped that the forty-mile bus trip into Aberdeen might make me feel better. This was a decision made in Walking Wounded but somewhere between country and town I had moved down to The Pits.

Stung by being spotted I moved off and headed for the bus station via an indoor market food hall so that I could buy some fresh food. The baker was in front, the butcher to my right and the fishmonger to my left but here, too, I had become rooted to the floor. I would start to head for a counter but every time the attempt would be cancelled by some negative force which prevented me from continuing with the move. And on the battle went, a grown man unable to purchase a sausage roll.

I tried to gee myself up. 'C'mon, c'mon, this is ridiculous. There's no food in the house; you have to eat something. Tomorrow you will be looking for something to eat. Even a sausage roll will do. Get anything. Go to the butcher first. Get some bacon – you like bacon, c'mon.'

But it was no good; I stood there numb and miserable. Fully aware of my behaviour this time, I did make a purchase. Eventually, I shoved myself in front of the fishmonger and bought a small bag of smoked cod roe. Not exactly what my urgings had meant by 'anything' and certainly not the shopping I had intended to pack my rucksack with. But I slept on the bus home and did, as I hoped, feel better in the evening. I saw the joke the following day when back in Walking Wounded. I fed the cod eggs to the hens and ate their eggs instead. I dislike cod roe.

Seeing the joke is one thing, enjoying it is another; although sometimes, later in a day of despair in which thoughts of self-destruction may have dominated every moment, suddenly I notice that I have smiled in a conversation or laughed at something on the telly. I'll stand up and sing myself a bit of Sinatra and not want to go to bed but I know what is going to face me only an hour or two after I do, when I will wake up deep in tomorrow's nightmare. Whatever happens, happens very quickly; I know that this moment is merely a breather and offers only a few hours' respite.

This 'feeling better in the evening' phenomenon confuses your observers. Try sharing with someone that you are going through a bad depression when you seem (and at that moment, are) in good form. It certainly used to confuse me.

'I find that a good walk clears my mind,' say some self-helpers. I am truly pleased for them but it is not so easy as that for some of us. Living, as I do, in the countryside I just have to step outdoors to be somewhere pleasant but time after time I have dressed for an attempt at break-out just to return minutes later, stymied by a depression which would only let me shuffle about at the front gate, unable to decide which direction to go. Here I am, the hardy outdoors man – the rock climber, the solo sea canoeist, the guy who backpacks off-route in the wildest of the Scottish mountains – not able to get past the front gate.

And there is pain in moments like these. I mean physical pain. Pain that wrings through my body when foolishly I attempt to take on the depression by some physical means: baking, weeding, a shower, cleaning my teeth.

One of the toughest things I have done in my life was to creosote the byre doors whilst in The Pits. The tactic was to do something that needed to be done, which would please me to view it afterwards but which would not take that long to achieve. But just changing clothes for the job was a torture as my body screamed to be left alone. Somehow I finished the job – all three byre doors. Slapping the creosote on at the frantic rate I worked, it only took an hour. With every dip, drip, stroke and stink of the stuff I wanted to run away and end the pain, to get back to the tunnel which I should never have left.

I am sure that forcing the pace like this can only do some of us harm. If I have managed to shower or go for a walk I feel that it is not because I have risen above my depression and have courageously done something to help myself, it is because the depression in its own time has lifted enough to release me – then a shower and a walk is possible and will make me feel even better.

Music helps some sufferers, although not always me. I sat in the best seat of the house once whilst the Royal Scottish National Orchestra performed a wonderful Scandinavian rhapsody. I hardly heard it. On that night the music played in two venues: in one place to a spellbound audience in Aberdeen's gorgeous Music Hall; in the other it was merely background accompaniment to the malignancy that boiled within an outsider's mind. I was a hospital in-patient at the time and, on reflection, I guess I could have picked a more suitable programme that night than Sibelius and co. I would have been far better in the hands of Elkie Brooks who was also live in town that week. Yes, her *Knights in White Satin* and a fish supper on the way back to the ward might have worked something for me.

1st Concert Goer

>Wisn't the violin concerto jist sublime?

2nd Concert Goer

>Well, my concentration was a bit off tonight. But it did form an interesting, even dramatic, background to the planning of a series of revenge murders, torture, arson and public humiliations which I've had in mind for some time.

1st Concert Goer

>Aye, 'at's Shostakovich for ye.

I tell myself that as long as I can see the jokes I will be all right. Nothing can stop these depressions leading my thoughts into the darkest of places, but when I am able to I remind myself that this is my illness at work. It is the illness that produces this useless, disabled version of me. That it *is* me is a thing I accept, but it is far from being the best of me and, although every depression is a new nightmare, so far the fairground car has always made it out into the sunshine again. Stepping off the ride and walking out of the park altogether would be a fine thing but that does not look like ever happening.

3

Lost in Fife – The Beginning

I was twenty-four years old and eighteen months into my first job as a youth worker when things started to go seriously wrong. Until then it had seemed to be a great two years with no repetition of any extreme manic episodes or depressions such as I had experienced as a student. I do recall vague feelings of unease at some obsessive behaviour but I was not at all what you could call a reflective person in those days. Cheered on by my ferocious work rate I was delighted just to view myself immodestly as a gifted, super-energetic and dedicated youth worker. Only once was there a warning that something might be wrong: a colleague took me aside at a party and said that I should slow down, that I was burning myself out.

And slow down I did when I was struck with pericarditis, an inflammation of the heart and found myself laid out and helpless in the medical ward of a general hospital. Once I was over the first unpleasant couple of days, I settled nicely into the role of model patient. It was a new, comfortable hospital in which the nursing staff were attentive and friendly (one nurse used to give us all a kiss before she went home at night – things have changed I think!). There was nothing to it really; I did not have to undergo any unpleasant treatments, I did not think I was going to die any more and my friends and work colleagues made a great fuss over me. I just lay back and waited happily to get better, which in two weeks I did. However, a second inflammation hit me and I was re-admitted, but now a dramatic change had taken place in my head. Suddenly I was the model patient no more. Although I was quite ill and, as before, the treatment was complete bed rest, I could not stay in bed. Not that there was anywhere to go in that small medical ward but just to sit in the privacy of the toilet or cool myself down in a cold shower was a release. I'd be found, be told off by horrified staff then returned to bed; but after an hour I would have to be up and moving around again. Patients have always sneaked out of hospital beds but the nursing staff soon realized that this was not the usual sport. At night, in spite of the sleeping pills I was given, I hardly slept – here was another sin held against me as the staff's dismay at my behaviour increased.

It was a hypomanic attack and desperately confusing. I did not know what was happening; I had no control at all over my behaviour and suddenly all my nice nurses were hating my guts. Finally a nurse coming on shift found me relaxing in the hospital's outdoor fountain. They dried me off and I was fortunate to be seen by a clever doctor who came and spoke to me for some time. Would I speak to a colleague of his, a psychiatrist? Obviously, he had a hunch.

I guess that moment when a psychiatrist is first suggested to you is pretty well branded in your memory. Shrinks are one of those things that mental cases need – loonies, head-cases, other people, that is, not people like me.

The psychiatrist *I* needed appeared a day later and after a brief chat hit me with a dose of thioridazine – turning me into a form upon which the nursing staff could do their work. This drug, a powerful anti-psychotic, plus the sleeping pills that appeared, were the start of a prescription drugs problem which was to complicate my manic depression wonderfully; but maybe my doctors from that time can be forgiven for not looking that far ahead. After being discharged from hospital, my manic depression still undiagnosed, I made the first of many long visits to The Pits. Confused and unable to return to work I sat up night after night in my flat trying to understand what had turned my world upside down. In the next eighteen months the situation was to get worse. I had a collection of pills that became more colourful after every surgery visit, had a course of ECT (Electro-convulsive Therapy), attended a day psychiatric unit and had been an in-patient at a psychiatric hospital (the 'Flaming Buckets' hospital described in the next chapter). I plagued church ministers, frequently phoning them up at late hours. I was a telephone Samaritans regular, I cut my wrists, took prescription drug overdoses. At work, where I had had long absences, I was now an embarrassment. An insomniac, a hypochondriac, a prescription drugs abuser, I was in a bit of a mess.

In this state I got myself up north to my parents' home in Aberdeen and after making contact with the psychiatric service there, was admitted to my second psychiatric hospital in six months. I had come to the right place; my collection of pills was removed and within days I was sleeping like a log without them.

Maybe it had something to do with the coal fire that burned at one end of the ward or the night nurse who looked like somebody's grandfather, but whatever the chemistry was I was to sleep like this for the rest of my stay there. I cannot remember how long I was a patient at this hospital, maybe three months. Negative memories include milkless custard and the parting consultation I had with a psychiatrist whose diagnosis was that I was just a 'bit immature'. I am sure I was but I rather think that I was a bit manic-depressive too. But he sent me back to Fife in good shape and although depressions and manic episodes were to continue to frequently complicate and interrupt life, it was to be a while before I was to become so ill again. If any of the doctors I had encountered in those first years suspected I had manic depression I was unaware of it. The only clear description I ever got was from my GP: 'Recurring moderately severe depression.'

But life was sweet again and I was back in town to see what was new. I found a new job as a residential child care worker, made new friends, met the woman I was to marry. There was plenty to be getting on with.

4

Flaming Buckets – Seventies Psychiatric Hospital I

If you had been driving past the Admission Ward building, in the grounds of a southern Scottish psychiatric hospital one particular afternoon in the summer of 1973, you would have seen a rubbish bin with smoke rising from it sitting outside the front entrance. Then you would have seen two men in white coats run outside, pick up the bin and run back inside with it. 'What the f...' you would have said.

The Admission Ward building was a relatively new one, maybe early sixties. The place I lived in consisted of a large, square, high roofed room divided into two areas by a glass partition. On its scuffed, unpolished floor stood thirty-odd beds with their bedside lockers, a large table in the centre with games and magazines stacked on it, assorted chairs and a large swing-top bin beside a sink. I remember large windows admitting plenty of light but cannot remember if they had curtains or blinds. People smoked where they liked in those days and so scruffy ashtrays lay all around. It was not a very nice place to live but I had become half used to it.

It was a hot day and after another stodgy lunch several patients were lying sleeping or, like me, just lazing about on their beds. I smelt burning and looked across to see smoke rise up through the lid of the bin a few yards away. As usual there were no nursing staff present in the room. I investigated. The bin was on fire all right and although there were, I suppose, other options available, I thought only to remove the bin from the ward without delay.

Being careful to avoid swinging the lid, I held it out at arms length and marched steadily out of the ward and along the short corridor that led to the main entrance. As I passed the ward office at the end of the corridor I glanced through the open door at the backs of the nurses (all male) and saw that, again, they were engrossed in showing their small millimetre home movies to one another. Without stopping I called out that the bin was on fire and, satisfied at the sounds of commotion behind me, kicked the main entrance door open and put the now seriously reeking bin down a few yards away from the building. I stood back to wait for my Brownie points.

Out rushed the aforesaid nurses. One whipped up the bin causing the lid to swing and admit oxygen (and so allowing the contents to flare up) whilst his mate held open the door to let him pass back into the foyer and on into the ward office where the burning bin was extinguished with electric kettles of water. I think that there must have been a wool jersey or some other equally smelly item alight in there because the consequence of the staff's actions was a stink that reached into every corner of the building, including mine to which I had retreated.

I got my Brownie points and an explanation a short time later when an embarrassed nurse sidled up. He thanked me and told me that I had done the right thing. He said that they had taken the bin back inside the building because there were 'too many eyes out there'. This was a relief because, in the condition I was in at that time, I felt that it was actually me who had done something really stupid.

If I had been even more ill, say a paranoid schizophrenic, I would have understood even better, even sympathized.

Nurse It was best to take the burning bin inside. There are too many eyes out there.

Paranoid Schizophrenic
   Hey, tell me about it.

I was marked down as troublemaker. A return to the ward in the early hours of the morning (the ward doors were locked at 9pm) followed the last mile by a crawling police car, earned me a legally doubtful 'confined-to-barracks'. Another time two unnecessary attempts to have my chest x-rayed failed. On the first occasion, horrified at the noise and the lines of all kinds of patients attending the monthly x-ray day, I turned and was out of that bedlam quicker then you can say 'breath in'. A month later, on the second attempt, I veered off and away from the humiliating, wordless, shuffling line of patients being led by a white-coated nurse across the grounds.

   'Come back here at once, Mr Adams.'

This ward had been my first introduction to psychiatric hospitals — on the second attempt that is. My first admission lasted about two minutes. I took one look at what seemed to me more like a dosshouse than a hospital and fled. But my doctor had me back a day later.

   Some of the patients were very ill and I thought they should have been better cared for. This was confirmed when a nurse new to the ward came on the scene. He was smartly turned out and had an experienced air about him. As always in the mornings I helped to get the less able patients up and assisted with the bed making, which I had learned to do as professionally as any nurse. As I worked with the new man I saw his concern rise as he discovered standards in the ward which were obviously below those to which he was accustomed.

   A few other decent nurses appeared on that ward. Men and women who would chat and play cards and go out with patients on strolls, etc. These were people who made you feel better for a short time but they did not seem to have much impact upon the prevailing standards in the place.

The putting green, however, was maintained to a very high standard. This was a rambling eighteen hole affair created on the extensive lawns that surrounded the building. This was a patient facility, of course, but the nursing staff's enthusiasm for the green was obvious. Following daily inspections there were days on end when, to avoid damaging the green, no play was allowed. Not that patients wanted to use the putting green all that much but the ongoing staff versus patient competition did provide a means of meeting nurses who hitherto one had only seen reading the newspaper in the ward office.

I, however, came from a golfing family and smelt a rat. Perhaps all of this was appropriate but somehow I felt that we, the patients, were being used. Maybe it was the ruthless hidings we suffered in these competitions, possibly it was the superior putters that the staff played with, it could have been the golfing mags that lay around the ward office; I dunno, maybe I am just a bad loser, but I had the strong impression that the staff were keen golfers.

Having only had experience of a general medical ward for comparison, I thought that the poor care and seediness of the ward was standard for psychiatric hospitals. A short visit one day to the women's ward adjacent disabused me of this notion. It was very nice: no dirty ashtrays, there were rugs here and there, the floor was polished and they had spider plants and other nice touches about the place.

What was going on in my ward then? I discussed this experience later with friends who had nursed at this hospital and who knew about that particular ward and so I now know that the whole of the hospital was not like this. It was just a bunch of guys getting away with doing very little work, that's all.

I wrote a comic article for the hospital's newsletter about how as a volunteer driver during the ambulance strike the previous year, I had driven a patient in an ambulance to the very ward I was now a patient in. Astonishingly, although they said they were desperate for articles, they did not use it.

5

Pay and Free Uniform – Seventies Psychiatric hospital II

Not much was done for me in my months at the NHS school for golf and bucket fire control and, as described in Chapter Three, half a year later I found myself led into the acute ward of another psychiatric hospital. This was the place with the coal fire. The ward was located in a wing of one of the mostly attractive granite buildings called 'villas' which were scattered throughout the old asylum's spacious grounds.

Here the formality of a former time in psychiatry was still, to some extent, to be experienced. In that long room no arrangement of the beds other than the two rows along each wall was possible but it was, compared to the previous NHS effort, the Ritz. To begin with it was clean and at the far end of the ward there was a pleasant airy sitting area to which a nurse led me on arrival. There was also that coal fire and its night shift keepers.

Only a few years previously the hospital had operated a farm and in the mid-seventies work therapy/work ethic was still an important part of the hospital's systems; the ward, therefore, was empty of patients until the hour came when they returned from their various activities.

The patter was good. Staff and patients sat back and laughed at this and that and I got my first taste of the atmosphere I was to live in for the rest of that summer. This was a far more professional set-up. Here, in this ward, none of the poor standards that prevailed in my previous accommodation were to be detected anywhere. My main memories here are of the friendliness of the staff, the coal fire, the bowling greens and the pleasant rural location with its spacious grounds and gardens. The hospitals we see now have *landscaping* – this hospital had *gardens*.

I still look back on all of this with gratitude although I was not too impressed when, in my second week, the industry manager showed a dozen of us a huge pile of old telephones with the invitation to strip them to bits by way of a therapeutic activity. My withdrawal took place without discussion; I simply walked away.

But the staff persisted in their attempts to get me into gainful employment and, keen to avoid the work sheds, I found myself a post in a psychogeriatric ward – higher-status employment which I felt was much more my style. In this job I wore a tie and a crisp white coat in which I was delighted to be taken for a doctor sometimes as I flapped my way to and fro across the grounds to my workplace – yes, this was definitely me.

At first, though, the ward was a shock. Behind the walls of the handsome building in a corner of the hospital's verdant lands I stepped into a world of urine, excrement, hopelessness and seventies Radio Two. I stuck it though; two hours in the morning and two in the afternoon for which I was paid a useful sum so I suppose you could say other people's bodily wastes had become my daily jam.

In no time I got accustomed to the stench, the bodies I washed every day and the mute, unknowing faces I shaved and fed. Sometimes, though, I could draw a smile; short tiny smiles but worth the bother. I soon became as cheerful as the ward's nursing staff about it all. The place was described as a 'terminal' ward – all of these people were here to die but nearly all had already left us. Our job was to keep them clean.

The nursing staff treated me as one of the team and gave out bits of the patients' backgrounds: *he* had been a headmaster; *her* husband had a big building business; *he* had been manager of a famous football club; *she* had only come in with depression. Gee, thanks for telling me!

It was an exhausting ward to work in and my admiration for the staff was considerable but a disgraceful incident was to reveal a wart in their midst. One day I turned, startled, when I heard a nurse call out angrily and saw him trying to get an unwilling patient out of a chair. To my astonishment the nurse grabbed the patient by his jersey and roughly hoisted him to his feet. The patient howled and God knows what he thought was happening to him next when his carer dropped him on the floor. There were other nurses in that room and they also took in that tableau of a white-faced nurse standing over a demented old man lying frightened and helpless on the floor. At least I hope that is what they saw.

Nothing was said. A nurse went over to help her struggling colleague and everyone went back to what they had been doing. At our tea break the nurse was his usual, sociable, Kit-Kat munching self and the patter round the table was as jolly as ever. The assault, it seemed, had never happened. Somehow, I felt that this was not the first time that an incident like this had never happened.

One day I was taken for some personality tests and although the psychology I had done at college was very basic, I recognized them all, particularly the Rorschach Ink Blot Test. I found it disturbing as a student and did so again here. A female medical student under the supervision of a female doctor gave me the test – I couldn't possibly tell her the things I saw in the cards and made up some of my responses. Maybe this is where the psychiatrist got his 'immature' from.

More tests followed. I was taken on the daily minibus run to the city infirmary for a brain scan although I was told only that I was going in for a 'test'. On arrival at the hospital the driver looked at his lists and shouted for 'Brian Scan'. After several blank-faced responses a nurse sorted it out and everybody had a good laugh at my name and my scan. Everybody except normally cheerful me. I had not been told much about why I was going in to the infirmary that day. It had never occurred that there might be something worth scanning my brain for. There wasn't.

As previously mentioned, the going away diagnosis given at this hospital was: 'bit immature'; and so, pleased that there was nothing really wrong with me and that all I had to do was grow up, I cheerfully went back to my flat in Fife and back to my work as a youth leader.

The diagnosis was rubbish. I was to learn far more about manic depression now than I knew then (which was nothing), but looking back on my behaviour there, I suspect that the staff missed or misunderstood my restlessness and the ways in which I constantly strove to extend my boundaries. Getting myself the job in the geriatric ward was an example. Other activities included organizing lawn bowling tournaments and representing my ward at patient council meetings (once taking my milkless custard up to the kitchens for an explanation on behalf of my constituents).

During a particularly restless period, secret activities included entering, by way of drainpipes and unlocked first floor windows, the hospital's unoccupied villas. There is nothing emptier than a mothballed hospital ward. Rows of bed frames, a stack of mattresses and that is it. Not so much as a nail brush in a building which for decades had been full of life. One exception was a villa equipped with a full-sized snooker table. Surrounded by the silence that had followed me there, I resisted setting off the clack of snooker balls.

6

Talking to God – Suicide

There are periods of time when every day I wake up and my first conscious thought is: 'Oh, no.' Centuries of human beings have experienced this despair in the hells of slavery, imprisonment, persecution and abuse. Although I experience it from a warm bed, I still, nevertheless, experience it.

When my heart sinks at the prospect of another day of being me, I am usually in a condition in which wherever I go I view all high fittings from the point of view of their ability to hold a rope with me at the end of it. Whether this means I am suicidal or obsessed with suicide, and whether there is a difference, I do not know.

How close have I been to topping myself? Once I was so crazed that I thought I had just done it and that back in the byre the physical me hung from a rope. But how close have I really been to the act: a year away or five minutes, a wrong word, a crisis? A just too unpleasant thought, a final, unshakeable, gut-twisting flashback?

The problems of suicide, always the same ones, run through my mind like an endless tape: the effect it would have on family and friends; how to do it properly; how to minimize the unpleasantness for everybody.

In the elevated state I enjoy at the time of writing, the thought of self-destruction is far from my mind and my view of suicide is that its contemplation by a person suffering from depression is a symptom of their illness and that they should be locked away for their own protection. Next week I will tell you that doing away with a life spoiled by depression and any other cruel illness for that matter is the right thing to do, that western society's objection towards suicide is just a flabby cultural taboo.

There is one egotistic version of me that finds it difficult to consider being absent from the world's proceedings; my not liking the thought of being dead and everybody else being alive and going about the world as if there was nothing wrong. Then there is another version – more humble, more deadly, one that couldn't give a monkey's for any of that, one where it is just a matter of picking the right time to exit.

I recall a statistic that said twenty per cent of manic-depressives do kill themselves. That being so, manic depression is a potentially terminal illness – I'd guess that many cancers have a better survival rate than that.

What helps is that as the comfortable atheist I have been for a couple of decades I have no fears of any existence whatsoever after this one. I reckon.

Atheist	Have I had an accident?
Angel	Yes.
Atheist	Am I in hospital?
Angel	No.
Atheist	Are you a nurse?
Angel	No.
Atheist	So where am I then?
Angel	Heaven.
Atheist	Oh shit!

In that first difficult period in the early seventies I did believe myself to be a Christian which, I think, means that I was. In the depths of another crazed period it seemed that death was very close. There, in my flat on the fourteenth floor, all I had to do was step outside. In desperation I got on to my knees and prayed to God for help.

Suddenly the answer came and my torment was replaced with joy and excitement when I was told what all this suffering was for, why I was put on this earth. God told me that I was here to save mankind by giving up my life. As a result of my death a person who was about to die would live in my place. This person was going to save mankind but it could only be done through my sacrifice.

I asked God about this person: How were they going to save mankind? Was he or she a scientist, a doctor? Was some threat to the planet going to be avoided by this person who was going to take over from me? How was I to die? When would it happen?

'Look,' God said, 'don't you worry about all that. I'll get back to you.'

At last my suffering was over. I telephoned a minister in Aberdeen with whom I was in touch to give him the good news. He was unconvinced, kept repeating that I had to 'be positive'. He said he would phone me later in the day.

Minister's Wife
> Who was that at this time of the morning?

Minister   Brian Adams.

Minister's Wife
> Oh, the guy with the flares?

Minister   Aye – thinks he's Jesus.

Minister's Wife
> God, nae anither een.

Me being ungrateful. In fact I recently found the kind letter that the Reverend wrote to me in which he refers to my 'death wish' period.

When you are in a condition like this, coincidence is no help at all. At another bad time after another crazed go at God, I got off to sleep at dawn. The doorbell rang at about ten in the morning and there, in their white shirts, stood a couple of Mormons.

'That was quick, God,' I thought, though it may have been: 'God, that was quick!'

'Come in lads,' I said, 'I've been expecting you.' (Not Mormons specifically, but that's God for you.)

They were delighted with me and spent the rest of the day drinking my orange juice and showing me pictures of prophets to prove everything they had to say. It turned out there was a crowd of Mormons (all from the USA) in the town at that time and so started a friendship with a great bunch of guys who helped me out of that suicidal hole and who improved my basketball game no end as well. As for the serious The Church of Jesus Christ of Latter-day Saints side of things, I read the *Book of Mormon*, which I still have, and listened to everything they had to say but I was never going to believe that version of God, even if He had sent them along to see me.

7

Christopher Columbus, David Livingstone and Me – Work

Every job I have ever had in the last twenty-seven years has ended in tears. No leaving presentations, no farewell drinks with the boys. I have never left a job to take up another. I know it looks bad. Twenty-seven years is the length of time I have suffered from manic depression. Before that my work record was quite respectable, starting age fifteen as a bakery van boy in that pre-oil Aberdeen of 1960.

'Baker! Baker!' I would cry up granite tenement lobbies. Within days I had developed my own particular swagger and vocal style, stretching the first syllable the length of the ground floor lobby then cracking the rest up to the second, third and fourth floors with a sharp, strangled glottal stop: 'Bayyyyyyygki! Bayyyyyyygki!' A frightening experience this if you were a stranger on those stairs when I burst in. A few streets on and the clientele were wifies from posh, gardened bungalows but even here the cocky van boy entered with hardly a knock, just like a doctor really.

On other, more gentle rounds I would carry mountains of pan loaves into Aberdeenshire farmhouses where often the driver had a cup of tea organized. There, after the bit of a fuss over new me was over, I sipped my tea and listened to the warm cleck* in kitchens where you could spend the rest of your life.

I worked for the Northern Co-operative Society which at that time was a well-established concern in the north east of Scotland. Later it tried to hold its own against the big supermarket boys but it went defunct. Maybe it was always going to be that way. When I first started the transport supervisor used me for holiday cover. Twice he allocated me to rural rounds but when I went looking for the vansmen I discovered that they were on their mid-week day off. I liked the sound of that – on the city rounds you only got a half-day off during the week. The first time this happened other (highly amused) vansmen took time off from loading their pies and cream buns to introduce me into the ways of that sixties Co-opie. They advised that, technically, I too was entitled to the day off. No, I should not go to see the transport manager – I should scram before he saw me vanless and tried to do me out of my rights by putting me on another van for the day. I was out of the loading bay before you could say 'custard slice'. I reckon the Co-opie's fate was sealed away even back then.

Much as I loved this life I could not be a van boy for the rest of my days and, as arranged, after eighteen months on the road, I was called in to start my five-year apprenticeship as a baker and confectioner. The bakehouse was a shock. Over was the freedom of the road, the sunshine, the snow, and the tips off wifies from Premnay to Portlethen. No more carry-ons with the shop quines; that black-haired lass in the Mastrick branch would have to take up with the next 'van-loon' to come at her with a cream bun. Paradise lost to the noisy, hot, dusty, seasonless incarceration of the bakehouse. But, as

---

*   Talk or gossip (Scottish).

we said then, 'it was a trade' which, at that time, for somebody like me was important.

Five years later at the age of twenty-one the RAF seemed a way out but within a truncheon's width of my joining up as a military policeman, one bit of good luck after another led to my running a youth hostel in the Scottish Highlands instead.

You meet all kinds of people as a youth hostel warden and as a youth hosteler you meet all kinds of wardens. I was the kind of warden that looked at the students who hitchhiked to my castle and thought: 'I want to be one of them.' From that mind-opener it was back to Aberdeen where my parents fed me for six months while I studied for the qualifications needed to train in the Youth and Community Service. In the autumn of 1968 I packed my blue-grey suitcase (an RAF going-away gift from my sister) and left with it for a different kind of life altogether as a student in Glasgow. I wonder what the RAF would have done with their manic-depressive policeman?

Since my Glasgow days and my first serious manic attack I have had eleven jobs, three of them in self-employment. In one I put in a respectable seven years but the average length of time spent in the others was twenty-two months. I have been sacked once, left to fade away once, resigned due to being pissed off twice and given up due to my manic depression four times.

It will be of no consolation to the officials involved in the above to learn only now of these statistics. They could, of course, have used them to improve the case for dumping me, not to mention their value as a means of not employing me in the first place. Perhaps, also, the bastards might have felt even more justified in doing what a bastard's got to do if they had known that others had been there before them – that they were in a story.

My first job in community work was as a youth leader attached to a secondary school. To have a youth leader based in every school in the county was the pioneering idea behind this and a pretty daft one it was too but I was not to know that and went at it with the enthusiasm which was to characterize every job I was to have. 'Brash' was my boss's description of me but he put up with it and I liked him. I felt I was making a difference to his school and every now and then he would agree with me that I was.

The devastating period of illness and hospitalizations I described in Chapter Three put an end to my time at the school but after my recovery I negotiated a transfer to the post of houseparent at a residential school for children who were then referred to as 'maladjusted'. Like me, some of the staff were in a bit of difficulty too. Although I was promoted to senior houseparent and it looked for a while as if I had found my true vocation, the headmaster and I were not to get on. It went crazy when I was sacked on no grounds at all. It was an awful business. For a while it looked as if somebody could have achieved my destruction by snapping his fingers. But the affront to myself and that of the school staff who had supported me was swept away when the council's lawyers slunk back from the industrial tribunal to which I had appealed and won. The tribunal found that I had been unfairly dismissed and awarded me £5000.

I kept clear of local government for a bit after that, by which I mean I started up a toy manufacturing business. With supreme gusto and a few brilliant ideas I lost most of the five thou' in no time at all – although they were quite good doll's houses. After a second attempt at financial suicide with a grocery van franchise I seized at a second opportunity to fit in with local government when a different district council advertised for a community worker and gave me the job.

I had learned a lesson; it was going to be difficult surviving the last quarter of the twentieth century by my wits alone and I was pleased to lodge in another local authority nest – at least for a while. At times I could make cracking good doll's houses and sell them no bother and at times I could be a brilliant grocer too but the problem was obvious – there was no way this bipolar could keep up self employment, or anything, day in and day out.

Once, though, maybe I could have shone with my moods and restlessness. Is this safe, pension-planned, insured, assured age a disaster for us manic-depressives? Was there a time when a manic-depressive was the thing to be?

I fantasize that back in another life my manic depression was a great success. An age in which I buccaneered at some concern that was not run by superannuated officials. More a Columbus or a Livingstone than a van Gogh or a Napoleon (all said to have been manic-depressives), I am cut off from executive control and all my manic-depressive attributes – super-abundant energy, vision, courage, enthusiasm and charisma – can be fully expressed. Amazingly the job with this district council turned out a bit like that. This was the job that lasted seven years.

Their Planning Department needed a community worker to help sort out a nasty little mess of urban decay in a small council housing estate. Without asking for references from my last and still smarting former employer and, taking my doctor's word for it that my health was fine (he wasn't that keen to say so), they did the right thing and gave me the job. It was a perfect situation: my bosses were based in the comfort of their offices while I was nicely isolated thirty miles away; they were town planners with their hearts in the right place but I was the pro at community work; I lived on the run-down estate, they certainly did not.

Fitting in with all of my brother officers went out the window in the first week when I exposed and articulated what was in my opinion the basic truth: the housing problem had been created by the council not by the tenants. An estate that had aged only a little had, through an antiquated housing allocation system, been used as a colony for people who did not care much about where they lived or had no choices about where they lived. What had started as an informal practice had soon become institutionalized; an unstated but deliberate social policy.

In this dumping ground the best of people, particularly single parents, struggled to keep their heads up, only to be treated with contempt by the very people who had created their predicament in the first place. Then the misconception that the community had inflicted the mess they lived in upon themselves gave the council's managers and elected councillors the permission they needed to perpetrate another unstated policy, another crime – that of negative discrimination. Instead of giving the area the extra resources it needed, it got much fewer.

It was not a contractual requirement that I live on the estate but in a typically reckless fling, I moved my wife and our bits and pieces into the meanest and most miserable example of sixties tenement building imaginable. My neighbours were as interesting as any on the estate but, apart from a few hairy nights, it was not so bad. My residency was a powerful tool, giving me authority in my dealings with the council and an access to the area's residents I could never have hoped to have achieved by dropping in during office hours only. I was not a council official, I was their neighbour and in many cases I was also their friend who shared the same humiliations they experienced and felt the same pain and anger. There was also that unfashionable thing in community work that I was happy to be when it was called for – a leader. I was never to lose the head start that staying on the estate gave me.

My marriage, though, had been struggling for some time and had come to an end. It says something about me that only now, a hundred years later, do I wonder why. The grim tenement and estate I had moved us into was certainly no way to treat a lady but our difficulties had started before this. Swapping the pantiled cottage in the tiny village we lived in for the town's worst to get me into community work seemed like a way forward. But the move, I think, could have been to anywhere. I was an undiagnosed manic-depressive and, as I still am, impossible to live with. You can't blame your psychosis for everything but as I look back on my erratic behaviour – the stunts, the enthusiasms, the carelessness with money etc. – I believe that Margaret was as much a victim of manic depression as I was. It was not just one of those things. She left on the day I started work on the estate and I never saw her again.

A whole range of problems festered in the estate and, although untidy gardens were the least of them, part of my strategy was to encourage and help individual tenants to make an effort to improve the look of their own corner. One day a wee girl from a particularly poor family came to my door and asked if I would repair her grannie's new mower. I was delighted. Here was another family responding to my irresistible charisma. She brought the mower to me for repair and I recognized it straight away – it was my mower! Somebody had pinched it from my shed during the night and sold it on to poor Grannie!

I loved all of this stuff and tore into the job with enormous enthusiasm and energy. Stepping far outside the bounds of mainstream community work – not to mention the odd ethic or two – there was little I would baulk at in my efforts to achieve the objectives set by my department and the area's residents, plus a few I had thrown in myself. Risk taking was my daily bread and I partook of it with relish although there were officials from other departments and some local councillors who would have been happy to see me choke on it.

Then an old unwelcome relative moved in to stop the fun.

Christopher Columbus, David Livingstone and me, eh? I wonder if they soared too. I know what they were when their power had flaked away and there came that moment when they realized that they were cursed with depression again. Columbus, becalmed and doubting, staring for days at the knots in the timbers of his cabin roof or Livingstone weeping for no reason at all in some hot, humid tent.

In a tenement flat in Scotland with everything going for me again, there came that moment when I realized that an old, unwelcome version of myself had moved in to stay for a while. Churchill called it his 'Black Dog'.

The doctor said that the break-up of my marriage had caused the upset but I just recognized another depression. The truth was that the day after the final ending of my marriage, I was back into the fray as if nothing had happened. Years were to pass before I was to mourn the loss of what Margaret and I should have had, and then a decade before I realized how selfish I had been and felt any responsibility at all. My self-centredness had been total – I had never once given a thought to my marriage or to her.

I was still undiagnosed and knew nothing of the chemical thing that was happening in my brain, all I knew was the powerlessness and anguish of not being able to understand why I was now hiding from, and repelled by, the streets which yesterday I strode with such confidence. With the ingenuity of the alcoholic hiding his drinking, I hid my disabling depressions and for the second time in my life, this time as a thirty-something, I went looking for help from a psychiatrist.

More serious ups and downs followed at work. Sometimes I was available for absolutely anything all of the time, and sometimes you could not find me for love or money; but I got away with it for seven years without ever being challenged. Over the piece, though, I believe that I was good enough value for money and that maybe given the risk taking involved the community worker in that job needed to be of the manic-depressive variety.

After four years, the council satisfied enough with their mostly rehabilitated housing estate (I was not), I was offered a further three year contract to work in other council housing areas which were thought to be in danger of decline. Although I guessed that it was a project that would end in tears, it was a challenge and with no other good career path ideas, I had a go.

The weaknesses of the council were well known to me by this time and, although I had been given a prevention remit, when it came to the bit and something special was needed, I expected trouble. It had been hard enough getting the system to address itself properly to its housing disaster in the estate I had just left, never mind getting it off its corporate backside for a try at preventing future disasters. The disgust I felt for the people responsible for these social messes was complete. A cure in council housing sickness is nothing to celebrate, it is not a cure at all; childhoods have already been spent and stigmatized in the squalor and shame of community decay.

Things went wrong early on with the new job. Mistakes I made did not help and it ended more with a whimper than with tears when eventually the last year of my contract was given over to me to do nothing with and keep out of harm's way with. The elected oafs who ran the council at this time, briefed by their much less oafish officials, decided that I would only undertake community work as defined by the council which was that I must not work with people in community groups!

Consider the breed that drew up that cynical cracker; local government servants pre-sliming the way ahead for their political masters. Nothing here, in my opinion, will ever change. Every employer I ever had needed people like these to protect their institution's particular brand of mediocrity. In government, trusts, quangos and the so-called non-profit making charities, achievement in terms of public benefit or a 'job-well-done' seems to be worth nothing whilst playing the corporate game is everything. There is a lot more to holding down a job in these places than just being good at it – not rocking the boat being the prime requirement. How is somebody like me going to do that?

Obsessiveness is the main attribute/problem of manic-depressives of my kind. Intense commitment and passion is invested in whatever activity is undertaken and towards whatever objective we are set upon. The pain we experience when some imperfection or barrier gets in the way of our goals is unbearable. This is difficult enough for friends and family to take, never mind nine to five work colleagues.

I doubt if bipolars can be corporate players at all. I remember spoiling it again for everybody when the word 'synergy' came up at yet another earnest self-reassessment of a team of which I was a member. 'Synergy' and 'team' concepts are still utilized by some social workers, community workers and the like who think that through the 'team', the total can be greater than the sum of its parts. My experience informs me that the team only exists at meetings of its ill-prepared members who could actually be out there doing the job instead of drinking coffee and writing pages of already forgotten minutes which somebody else on the public payroll is paid to type up and file. My plot theory instincts tell me that the team is not intended to be a means of producing excellence or of anything of a consumer-orientated sort. The team is required as a means of bonding, staff control and of passing away a few harmless hours.

I confess that wherever I went I always spoiled the team experience for my colleagues. I would say that it needed spoiling; they would say I was difficult to work with, which I was. Understandably, community workers do not like working with someone who challenges them with the theory that they are participants in a plot in which the real purpose of community work is to employ community workers.

Clearly, although I recognize the presence of genuine local government cock-ups in plenty, I subscribe firmly and enjoy much more the conspiracy view. That these are the ravings of one cast out from the club is, I agree, a possibility but if my view of local authorities and their like is a paranoid one then lock up every Joe and Jane on the planet. The conspiracy that is our public services is timeless, something that the public has always understood.

Our so-called public servants are in fact our masters and that the local authority industry they run is run for themselves. The raw material of the public service industry is not the consumer, the raw material is the industry itself, serving itself. The whole pseudo-mystical jing-bang called 'management' is how the the system looks after itself but which is its stock in trade also. All of it – the teams, the jargon, the management systems, the reorganizations, the public consultations, the complaints handling systems, etc. – is grist to a mill that exists for the millers, not for its so-called customers.

Institutionalized short-changing is where this industry's profits are made, the dealings in which we – patients, clients, users, pupils, students, members, tenants, tax-payers, inmates – are given our slice or crumbs of the cake in the way of services which can be bad, adequate or even very good but only after the people we think we employ have taken their share.

You really do not want me in your team, do you?

My 'plot' views on the nature of public and voluntary services at the time of my separation from them had not yet been worked up to that dark pitch and naively I put the time my employers had put at my disposal into creating other forms of it.

During my time at the first housing estate I put together the financial package to found its Citizens Advice Bureau (CAB) and at another posting worked with others to start a voluntary organization to work with families in areas of deprivation. Stuff which, at the time, I thought was crucial to mankind but which in the case of the CAB was immediately subverted into securing a retirement job for the local candidate (by a mile the least suitable) and on the committee more status for the busiest of the local busybodies. That CAB still exists though and indeed I had cause to ask for some advice from one of its advisors myself a year after I had put it together. Maybe I had just caught her on a bad day but I knew enough not to take her lousy advice!

My short career in journalism also started during this time. For several years my interest in wildlife conservation had been developing and in an idle moment (in your time, i.e. the time in which tax and ratepayers and community groups should have been getting the service of a community worker) I sat down to write an article on wildlife (badgers, as I recall) for a local newspaper. The editor paid me ten quid and asked for one every week. That led to more feature work. In half a year it had all fallen wonderfully into place. By the time I had finished my contract with the district council I was set up in a new trade as a freelance writer. Well paid news-gathering and broadcasting for a local radio station fell into my lap and my past employers were able to find out who had been taking the piss out of them in the spiky newspaper columns I wrote for two local papers – under a pseudonym, of course.

It was all very promising but now, without the monthly cheque that your public service managers were happy to send me every month, there was not quite enough in writing to pay the mortgage of the country cottage I had bought. What to do? Wage slave to support the mortgage or follow this new avenue that had opened up? No contest, I transferred my hostas and hens to a rented cottage nearby in the private country estate where I have lived for the last twelve years.

But the darkness drifted in and out again, finally to choke off the gift; I was unable to survive the depressions that had found me gasping to stay alive in the unforgiving world of freelance journalism. The crunch came on a Sunday night in the spring of 1987 when I realized that I was never going to complete a simple advertising feature job which until then I thought I was just putting off. The truth was that I could not face the typewriter even though it had been a breakthrough week in which a large, regional newspaper had used a feature I had sent them. Deep in The Pits, writing now repelled me and the loss of the career in journalism which might have been in front of me, now meant nothing at all. There were no regrets, nothing, nothing at all.

A couple of years of employment followed as a development officer with a wildlife conservation organization, which as a volunteer I had played a part in building up. Sadly, there was hardly a member of its management committee who did not, it seemed to me, have their own self-seeking agenda in almost all of their dealings within it and the crippling power struggles that got me down as a volunteer were to get me down as an employee too. I had to walk away and from a distance watch all that potential wither as, I see now, it was always going to do: the purpose of wildlife conservation managers is to conserve opportunities for wildlife conservation managers.

The group, though, did achieve some good along the way. Many trees were planted and it was also the means by which over forty miles of disused railway line was saved from being leased piecemeal to anybody who wanted to graze a horse on its banks. Shortly after coming to the area I had noticed the disused line and with others saw its potential as a walkway.

Saving the line for the community turned out to an even bigger challenge than it had first seemed which, of course, was right up my 'walkway' and that of a few others too. Neither the District Council nor the Countryside Commission would entertain the notion. It had been 'Brian Adams' pipe dream', a council director had the honesty to confess to me afterwards. Eventually, however, they all stood and smiled for the cameras when we opened the first small stretch of the walkway.

Now the walkway offers wonderful walks through the heart of the Aberdeenshire countryside from Aberdeen to Peterhead and

Fraserburgh. I recently wrote an article about the walkway for a prestigious north east magazine and got a decent earner out of it, which was only fair enough.

8

One of Us – Famous Manic-Depressives

Winston Churchill, Abraham Lincoln, Theodore Roosevelt, Robert E. Lee, Rab Butler, Albert Einstein, Michelangelo, Vincent van Gogh, Pablo Picasso, Beethoven, Tchaikovsky, Chopin, Mahler, Liszt, Berlioz, Schumann, Elgar, Mozart, John Ogden, St Francis of Assisi, Ernest Hemingway, Leo Tolstoy, Virginia Woolf, Graham Greene, William Cowper, Charles Dickens, Charlotte Brontë, Emily Brontë, David Livingstone, Lord Byron, Martin Luther, Dylan Thomas, Howard Hughes, Robert Burns, James Watt, Napoleon Bonaparte, Lord Nelson, Thomas de Quincy, Vivien Leigh, Elizabeth Barrett Browning, Isaac Newton, William Blake, Alfred Lord Tennyson, Edwin Landseer, Francisco Goya, Peter Paul Rubens, Paul Gauguin, Oliver Cromwell, Mao Tse-tung, John Keats, Robert Lowell, Brendan Behan, Charles Darwin, Florence Nightingale, Sigmund Freud, Marcel Proust, Mary Baker Eddy, Christopher Columbus, Spike Milligan, Baudelaire, Oscar Wilde, Samuel Taylor Coleridge, Edgar Allan Poe, James Turner, Lord Randolph Churchill, Sergei Rachmaninov, Alexander the Great, Gerard Manley Hopkins, Honoré de Balzac, F. Scott Fitzgerald, Eugene O'Neill, Hugo Wolf, Gioacchino

Rossini, John Ruskin, Dante Gabriel Rossetti, Lewis Grassic Gibbon, Mark Twain, Tennessee Williams, Hans Christian Andersen, J.M. Barrie, John Bunyan, Joseph Conrad, Alexander Dumas, Maxim Gorky, Kenneth Grahame, Henrik Ibsen, Henry James, William James, Charles Lamb, Robert Louis Stevenson, Samuel Johnson, Thomas Carlyle, Tony Hancock, T.S. Eliot, Oliver Goldsmith, Boris Pasternak, Ezra Pound, Shelley, Rudyard Kipling, George Romney, Wagner, Cole Porter, Irving Berlin, Noël Coward, James Watt.

This roll-call is created from the various lists of manic-depressive greats that float about in manic-depressive information packs. You may have spotted that the people on it are dead. There are lists of live ones too but, for the most part, greatness or even a decent talent appears to be lacking and so they are of little significance here except that, and please forgive my cynicism, I wonder whether one or two have not used their alleged manic depression to make themselves a bit more interesting.

Manic depression propaganda points to the likes of the late Spike Milligan, whose manic depression was well known, and the manic depressive greats who have gone before him, and poses the question: 'Where would the human species be today without manic depression?' The claim is, you see, that the world would be a less colourful, cultured and civilized place if there had been no such thing as manic depression – perhaps not even civilized at all.

This manic-depressive pedigree of mine is certainly impressive. The very pick of history's greats. When I was presented with one of these lists after my diagnosis I must say that it gave me a tremendous boost to discover the company I was in and, gladly, I swallowed the whole thing about my importance to society. Eventually, though, I came to feel some suspicion about these lists – I mean, where are history's nasties? Although we do have a few shifty characters on our books there is no Hitler, no Stalin, no Attila the Hun, no Ghengis Khan, Marquis de Sade or Vlad the Impaler on any of them. Perhaps the behaviour of history's real bastards is explained by some other, second-rate mental illness.

One wonders too about the credibility of the various diagnoses. The lists of history's manic-depressive worthies are claimed to be researched but we must wonder how, from here, the doctors or the bio-historians or whatever they like to call themselves can diagnose with any certainty Alexander the Great's alleged manic depression? It took six psychiatrists twenty years to spot that I was one and I was swinging from the chandeliers in front of them – maybe they were too busy with Alex's notes!

But although my feeling is that a pinch of salt should be taken when studying the manic-depressive halls of fame, there is evidence enough to show that many were indeed manic-depressives. 'So what?' you should ask; no doubt some of them had ingrowing toenails too! Surely many more creative types have been out there being brilliant, arty and charismatic and doing their bit for civilization without being manic-depressives, without being carriers of the so-called 'genius disease'.

The question begs to be asked as we study the lists of leaders, poets, actors, mathematicians, painters and writers: did those who were manic-depressives achieve their greatness because of their mental illness or did they achieve their greatness in spite of it?

Sir Winston Churchill's manic depression is alluded to in many accounts of his life but the suggestion (which I have heard made many times) that his illness played a powerful role in driving him through the Second World War and so helped to save Western civilization, is a bit creative. I am no historian but it does seem that one of Churchill's most important moments occurred when Britain stood alone and civilization needed a voice to stand up to the fascist threat. Here was a man who bravely snarled back at a terrible and seemingly invincible enemy when appeasement would have been the most popular thing all round. How tempting it is to postulate that Churchill's magnificence was the manic-depressive in him in full, confident, determined, charismatic, unrealistic flight.

Without having given Churchill's illness a moment's research I would guess that if indeed he were a manic-depressive, depression was the predominant feature of it. C'mon, you cannot have people with serious mental illnesses running, and winning modern world wars. We know about Churchill's adventurism and all that but if he had been as bipolar as me, and as hypomanic as I am at the time of writing, the Allied Invasion of Europe would have taken place in September 1939 – without any allies!

My guess is that Churchill's manic depression brought him mostly bouts of depression, bringing nothing of any good to him or to the war effort. His courage, stamina and adventurism were sourced not from the so-called 'genius disease' but from his basic character – in Churchill's case I am sure that his greatness was in spite of his manic depression, not due to it.

But in wondering whether manic depression can be of any good to an individual, I look at my own moments with hypomania and see that amongst the manic-depressive greats, it is claimed that there were many for whom their illness was of considerable creative significance to them.

Although some of my own creative produce has been powered in bouts of hypomania, this does not make me a Lord Byron or a Hemmingway. I may have walked in the same furnace as they did, that fearless place; possibly a talent-expanding place but also a place where you can make disastrous decisions or write (and no doubt paint or compose) pure rubbish. I cannot be the only manic-depressive in the world who has not emerged from a writing 'high' to have to dump pages of work which seemed at the time to be of great significance.

I have spent plenty of time with manic depression sufferers, both inside psychiatric hospitals and out. None of us felt like geniuses. The only arty type I have ever noticed anywhere was me and my 'artyness' is a very mild form of that affliction indeed! The most impressive sufferers I have met in hospital were farmers. I have never met anyone who saw any point in being a manic-depressive or who liked being a manic-depressive or anyone who would not have dumped their illness in a second if they could.

My experience tells me that no matter how powerful and creative the manic gifts can be, most, if not all of the manic-depressive greats, would, like the rest of the illness' sufferers, have cast away their affliction in an instant and been grateful to get on with their art and their lives unhindered by the misery of manic depression. Manic depression is not a fun illness. Like the rest of us, the manic-depressive greats experienced their illness as a pain in the arse – a force that weighed them down far more than a force that lifted them up.

9

Babes in My Moods – Paranoia

Just because you are paranoid doesn't mean to say that people are not out to get you. What is worse, being in a full-blown paranoid condition completely convinced that everyone and everything is out to get you all of the time, or having insight into your condition and desperately trying to hold on to your marbles by sorting out what is real and what is not? The latter was my experience for a short time.

Proof of a conspiracy against you does not always fall into your lap. The visit to the staff cans spoiled by overhearing your colleagues planning your downfall outside is mainly the stuff of television drama. To figure out what skulduggery is taking place against you, you need to use your head, your imagination as much as anything else. The trouble was that during a time when some people were certainly out to get me, my imagination was already working overtime.

A period of unemployment had followed my time in journalism and conservation and once over the novelty of being time-rich on the dole, I looked around again for some new ideas. But it was an old one that caught my eye: a community work post (not with a local authority), this time in an area of urban deprivation on an Aberdeen housing estate. Someone with the kinds of skills and experience I had in plenty was needed. With images of me striding heroically through another urban wasteland I answered the call and went from about £2000 per annum on the dole to about £15,000.

The job was with an established community project which employed half a dozen community workers. My responsibilities were in adult education, welfare rights advice and the production of a community newsletter. The project was funded by central and local government with the aim of supporting families with children. It is obvious that this can quite properly mean prioritizing work with women as indeed this project did.

Something else existed here though. All of the professional workers in the project were women but I felt that there was more going on than just the natural enough bias that a team composed of one gender only might be expected to extend towards their own sex. There were things about the project which I was never able to fully understand. It seemed to me that running underneath the project's worthy and usual enough, but uninspired, deprivation strategies, a female-oriented agenda was securely in place.

Not that this had resulted in any kind of sisterhood or bond between the project workers and their female clientele, most of whom were also involved in some aspect of the project's management systems. The opposite was probably more accurate. The problematic and sometimes chaotic lifestyles of the project-users were carried into the project's management. These proceedings were an unforgiving jungle in which jealousies, feuds and the self-interests of user-families and groupings dominated the often highly volatile and chaotic proceedings. My colleagues' feminism seemed to be an irrelevance in all of this and brought them more contempt than appreciation from many of their clients. In the same way a fisherman keeps one hand for the work and the other for the man, in this dangerous environment the community workers kept an eye on their backs and after a short honeymoon period so too did I.

I suspected that I had this tension between worker team and clients to thank for my getting the job. As hinted by the two interviews I had had to undergo, the selection process had been as problematic as mostly everything else in the project was. The committee knew well what the appointment of a male would mean to their all-female worker team; for one thing it meant not giving the job to the only other candidate – a woman who for some time had occupied the post on a temporary basis and had fitted in well with the team. So this put me in a difficult position.

As far as I could see, this worker had been doing all that was asked of her plus a bit more but it was my job now. Did I detect any unhappiness in my new workmates with my appointment? Well, let's see, taking the job of one of their colleagues I had moved into a well-established nest of essentially middle class, technophobic women all of whom were active members of a city women's organization. I was male, working class, middle-aged, assertive, experienced and had the office computer unearthed and whirring on my desk on my first day. In their office, in their face and in their lavvy – unwelcome? I felt about as welcome as a tink's lurcher at a cat show.

Other community projects with their particular slants on urban deprivation were based in the same building as ours. Here, within the ranks of these sister groups, I felt there existed some very unpleasant forces indeed, forces which were eventually to come down upon me. I should have been watching my flanks as well as my back.

My own colleagues, though, despite the tiny bits of nonsense they put my way were basically decent types; people who, in another situation, could quite easily have been my friends. But there was no chance of that here for the thing which the group as a whole had become, was not something I could easily live with. Little was being achieved and the way I saw it feminism had nothing at all to do with practical ways of bringing about change in the lives of the women and children trapped in poverty.

It seemed to me that the staleness of the project, its workers and its systems, was scandalous. In fact only a tiny percentage of our potential clientele were using the project. The stagnation was easily spotted: the same few faces appearing in the office looking for help or gossip or trouble; the same voices at meetings; the same issues being argued over; the same tensions; the same people monopolizing the project's precious resources. One or two users were genuine community activists but I saw how some of the the project's clientele were people who had become very skilled at accessing the resources available and who knew also how to protect this access. It became clear to me that the same level of underachieving also applied to the other organizations working in the estate. As I learned more about their operations, the dawning of how ridiculous the situation was gradually sunk in. They used our handful of customers too; all the projects more or less shared the same tiny pool of clients!

The projects, with the enormous expense involved (I estimated an annual wage bill of over half a million), had little to do with tackling urban deprivation; what it mostly had to do with was supporting the mortgages and careers of a colony of community workers who instead of helping a community had parasitized it.

I fancied that my fair play credentials for others were pretty well-established but I had never entered such a place before and, especially as the only guy, I was mostly on my best behaviour. But the feminism I saw here seemed a raw, unsophisticated thing. Germaine Greer it was not! All I could see was a group of professionals promoting one another and enjoying some kind of important experience by sharing little bits of power together.

For once I more or less used my head and in the same way that I would not talk religion with a Jehovah's Witness, I avoided any discussion of feminism here. I did, however, make various attempts to open discussion about the project's resources being spent on a small section of the community. But I was always shot down. The project they maintained *was* being effectual in the community.

This assertion had nothing to do with community work or feminism but had everything to do with a quiet life. The local tyrants who had been allowed to own the project would have to be taken on if the wider community were to be served and that was too problematic a task. All there was to do, I resolved, was to crack on with my own particular responsibilities and quietly attempt to develop strategies for getting in touch with the wider community.

And if I could have managed to play it cleverly like that I might still be in community work. What I did not need at that time was hypomania but along came an absolute roaster of a high. Quite handy in one way for beside this difficult work challenge I had also just started directing my first musical, *Brigadoon*, with a local musical society. In hypomania there was no lack of confidence; I had moved into as high a gear as any I had ever experienced. Fuelled by a manic high I was super-energized, irrepressible and invincible – both in show biz and, unfortunately, at work.

Only when it was over did I realize I had experienced a prolonged manic attack. My appalling driving alone should have had me locked away for my own and everybody else's protection. With my superior driving skills I judged every manoeuvre in my gleaming Rover with nerveless, silky perfection. I still shudder to recall how ruthlessly I drove: overtaking rows of cars, forcing oncoming drivers to move over if it seemed that there was plenty of room for three. Aggrieved motorists would flash their lights and offer me the entire vocabulary of one-handed gesticulations of which 'mad bastard' was the favourite. Completely unmoved by the bleats from these sheep, this goat sliced up and down that forty mile stretch from home to office and back, every weekday for four months – a man with a mission at both ends and, remarkably, getting away with it without scratch or penalty point.

Another clue was my behaviour in the production of the musical. No director will have set higher production values than I did on that show. The puzzlement of the cast as to what had happened to that nice man from the back row of last year's chorus, turned to various kinds of fear as I ripped into everyone and everything to achieve my artistic ambitions. Their director was in a place they could know nothing of. They did not know it and neither did I until a few weeks after the show when I realized full well where I had been as the exhaustion and depression moved in.

Now it was all change. From putting in an enthusiastic and fearless day's work I started arriving late and taking days off. From grudging the loss of three valuable hours by sleeping in them I was now sleeping my weekends away but still going to work unrefreshed on Monday mornings. With my mood declining my driving also changed but now I became an even more serious danger on the roads. Sure, I got in line and cruised along with everybody else; it was just that on the way home I would start to nod off at the wheel. Ever woken up to find that you are driving a car? If I had been a menace before, I was now a disaster waiting to happen both for me and the folk I was going to take with me

The pressures at work had become intense: fending off every-thing from minor humiliations to bizarre challenges became almost a daily experience. The incidents piled up. In one confrontation forced upon me at a team meeting, I was asked to realize that I carried out my duties 'as a man'. I thought I was carrying them out as a profes-sional community worker but, no, here I was 'in denial'. Perhaps not always being on my best politically correct behaviour did not help.

Boss Did you just call me 'babe'?

Me No.

Boss It sounded like 'babe'.

Me No, *'made'*, I said you got it *made*!

Boss Just don't ever call me 'babe'.

When the inter-worker problems started to appear relating to things I had said and was said to have said, it started to get very difficult. I was slow to catch on but eventually I realized that there were knives in my back.

About this time the paranoia started. There was certainly stuff going on behind my back, the trouble was that I started to feel that much more was happening than it was reasonable to believe. At team meetings I came to be convinced that my colleagues had met the night before in order to do me harm. This also applied to meetings at which the other participants were complete strangers to me. In city centre crowds, individuals of a particular type who I had never met in my life passed me by, but I was convinced that they knew fine who I was and that they had been put against me as well. In a quiet moment, by the fireside at home, I realized I was quite ill.

The most striking incident was one where I had been with a holidaying group of lone parents and their kids at a residential centre. The camp was going well and I was enjoying myself at it as much as the participants, but I had to leave one afternoon to drive into Aberdeen to attend a meeting of adult education workers. As soon as I entered the room the feelings of persecution hit me stronger than ever. I looked around and saw that everybody present was either glowering at me or ignoring me. Obviously, while I had been away at the camp, my colleagues had been at work behind my back; they had met with these people the previous night to help them prepare for the encounter with me. It would not matter what I said in the discussion to come, these people were all against me, the outcome had already been decided.

I wonder if I betrayed anything of my paranoia to them? In fact they were all there because of a breakthrough I had made in low-cost, single mum-friendly computer training and were all interested in co-operating to get it off the ground. Fortunately I was not chairing the meeting and, certain that I was going mad, I pleaded ill health (which, of course, was true) and rushed back to the safety of my deprived mums and kids at the residential centre.

I knew that all of this was crazy. What possible kind of threat could I pose to justify this persecution? How could every community worker, social worker and half of Aberdeen possibly be conspiring against me? But as much as I realized that I was paranoid, the feelings remained as powerful as ever. My common sense and the evidence I had, told me that at least some of the harassment I was getting was real and possibly even co-ordinated; but my head also told me that I was off my rocker. How to sort out the real from the unreal? Well, I had a bit of luck: I was able to have a good look at all I needed to know about what was happening behind my back.

Despite this and the support I had received from some project-users, I decided to give up the job. I had not been achieving much and at the end of one particular week in which I feared I was going to lose touch with reality altogether, I went into hiding. It was just too difficult and the absences from work just too embarrassing. I also realized that at the age of fifty the game was up; I would never work as a community worker or anything like it again.

A month after my resignation, following an independent consultant's report, the project was closed down by its funders due to its being ineffectual.

My colleagues had a point of view of course, and in looking back at the situation and trying to make sense of it, I start with the fact that I was seriously ill most of the time and not handling the team situation with any respect or tact or skill at all. Would any of them have noticed anything wrong, been able to spot my hypomania? I doubt it. Although I was certainly difficult to work with, this illness can take a bit of spotting. A string of doctors had failed to diagnose my manic depression, why should a bunch of community workers be able to? I do not think that they suspected for one moment that I was so ill.

The paranoia continued for about nine months after I resigned. I found that it mostly arose in Aberdeen crowds so I kept out of the city for a while.

What was the bit of luck that helped me sort out some of the facts? I got hold of the key to a particular filing cabinet for an hour and although, as they say, it was a damn close-run thing, I had a copy of the key made and the original back on its ring without the babes being any the wiser. Later I was able to take my time with the papers in that file. Much of what I needed to know was in there and so my information was good right up until the day I left. Was this, I wonder, a paranoid sort of thing to do or a man sort of thing to do?

10

Not Work, Not Working – Breakdown

I have worked in welfare rights, residential childcare, adult education and community work. Unemployment and poverty was not just something that happened to others, it was the grist to this professional's mill, my stock in trade. It is very hard to be the client. Exchanging a decent income for the state benefit I now receive is something that gets more worrying as natural wear and tear takes its financial toll on my bits and pieces; anxieties heightened in the case of really important kit. I look at this old word-processor which has been so liberating for me and wonder how I am going to replace it when it finally cashes in its chips.

As a community worker I remember calling on a woman, a single parent, to find her on her knees peering into the back of her washing machine with nothing but a butter knife to help her. Calling out a repairman was, on her income, out of the question. I found her courage very humbling and twenty years later it is an image that still inspires me.

When the financial realities of state benefit sunk in I sold my Rover for a Metro then my Metro for a motorbike then the motorbike for a decent mountain jacket. The Berghaus is good for the mountains and keeps the Scottish weather off my back for the walk along my track to the bus route.

No car then, no smoking, hardly a drink, no holidays and, at the time of writing, no woman. No takeaways or eating out except for a bit of Fraserburgh carrot cake in the church tea room. Luxuries are cinema, theatre and concerts. But even with a mild arts habit, what with that otherwise abstemious lifestyle and my concessions and all, I should be okay on my incapacity benefit, yes? Not really, poverty is how the recipients of state benefit are supposed to experience life. I have worked it out: in theory I should be able to save £11.50 per week. This is before health costs. I have just started £140 worth of dental treatment; that is about twelve weeks' savings. I need new spectacles. God help everybody else worse than me; single parents spring to mind.

Help from God and, at one time, help from me too. Without family or any other distractions I used to define myself as whatever I was paid to do. The loss of identity, power, status, challenge and purpose was as hard to bear as the financial loss. An unfriendly social worker once caustically referred to me as the 'People's Champion'. I was never that although I did enjoy wading in on behalf of people who for one reason or another needed help from somebody like me. I confess that although their gratitude was important to me, the thing I enjoyed most was the fight, meeting the challenge; and the bigger it was the better. Another thing I liked, I'm afraid, was the sound of my own voice. I know that none of this made me a nice person.

I made the decision to give up work after less than a year into my last job, the one with the babes. Sure it was a helluva job but I knew that once I could have done a lot better than I did. The writing was on the wall: my manic depression was crippling me; I would not work in community work again.

I took a week's leave to go for assessment with the local Employment Service Assessment and Counselling Team. The letter said to be prepared to attend between two and four days. I was out and back on the street in half an hour. My assessment had already been made: no retraining ideas or jobs for middle-aged manic-depressives had occurred to my embarrassed assessors. What did I expect, a magic wand waved to set me off on some new life-twist in a job where my manic depression would fit in perfectly? *Answer*: a pathetic 'yes'.

> 'Well, Mr Adams, we think that after looking at your psychological profile, work experience, life experience, interests, aptitudes, birthmarks, shoe size, the tea leaves, your psychosis and the general cut of your jib, we can confidently put you forward for training as Alexander the Great.'

I took off instead for a week to paddle about the Treshnish Isles off the west of Mull in my sea canoe. A gentle giant of a shark ignoring me gave me a fright; solo sea canoeing in the Atlantic fair takes your mind off things.

On Lunga I lay and watched the guillemots and puffins get on with it and remembered how I had finally been able to give up smoking on this people-less, grocer-less island when I had landed on it ten years previously. We were an expedition group of about fifteen from Fife. What were they all doing now? I know Kate started smoking again; John and Penny moved to Southampton then up to Orkney; Peter gave up the police and trained as a community worker.

We caught and ate rabbits, fished for fish and dived for crabs. Campfire every night, stories, singing, jokes. The songs we wrote we left behind when we had to leave this paradise.

The Atlantic was at ease that week, a millpond you could have skimmed over to St Kilda and back on. We spoke about that too but we never did it. I dived off Staffa's basalt columns into the mouth of Fingal's Cave – got a photie to prove it. You should never go back to a place where you had a time.

Guessing that there was not going to be anything new workwise around the corner, I approached the situation positively. My income on benefits would be permanently low but face it, I told myself, even when you were in the money you were always skint. Volunteering would compensate for the loss of a work challenge.

And for a while I looked good. I drove minibuses (yes, a manic-depressive driving minibuses!) for this and that organization and took over the running of the parish youth club; taking my country kids to Aberdeen for ice-skating, tenpin bowling and all that kind of thing. In an adult training centre I did some useful stuff with disabled folk on the production of a magazine. A community centre employed me as a tutor and I winged it impressively with creative writing and cake decoration classes – a diverse and powerful combination of skills that said everything about my history.

I had not done badly in my stage directing debut with *Brigadoon* but my involvement in musical theatre took off when I discovered a talent for playwrighting. I directed my first effort with a group I had started in my local village and then worked with them the following year on another. In 1998 I was a winner of the Mobil Scottish Playwrighting Competition with my play *The Pie Ring* and directed another play of mine *East of the Sun* with a local musical society after having directing *The Wizard of Oz* the year before. In 1996 *East of the Sun* was set to be produced and directed by me in His Majesty's Theatre, Aberdeen with a local cast. Besides this I had established a youth theatre group which had acquitted itself well and I was up to my neck in a rural theatre project which I had brought to lottery application stage. Over that first three-year period then, I was a useful, busy and apparently fulfilled person but manic depression does not care if you are in paid work or voluntary work – if it is time to rear its head, it damn well rears its head. It was depression time again.

Bit by bit the life I had built crumbled away. I was not handling the youth club well and quit after a night when I lost my temper with the kids and smashed a hockey stick against the wall to get their attention. A violent act, something that I had never done before. I withdrew from my volunteering at the adult training centre. The rural theatre project needed another two years of graft; it might have got there in the end but I had had enough of it and was glad to let it collapse

Half a dozen other projects fell by the wayside. Some people may have felt embarrassed at this decline but depression the illness, depression the anaesthetic. There was no pain experienced in this decay, no shame felt in the retreat, no disappointment at the dissolving of the useful world I had built around me, only relief when the phone finally stopped ringing and nobody wanted me anymore. Then I took a Stanley knife to my arms and face and climbed up on to the roof of my house to bleed.

I had been to the village pub with a friend for an informal music night. I sang a bit. At about 11.30pm I am dropped off at my cottage and am boiling the kettle for a cuppa. I feel fine – still singing. Suddenly I am clapping my hands together in wide swings, smashing the palms together as hard as I can: slowly, hard and uncontrollably. My hands sting then become numb. Now I am in the byre, putting a fresh blade into the Stanley knife and repeatedly slipping it down the length of my arms. Then I let my face have it. Nothing that needs a stitch, but plenty of red just the same. Although I am in a new and very strange place indeed I have the savvy to realize that while this cutting is relaxing and seems the right thing to do, I have certainly become a basket-case. On call that night was a doctor I knew socially – I had directed him in several plays. 'Steve,' I said, 'I think I have cracked up.'

At the cottage he demonstrated that in addition to his excellent bedside manner, his rooftop skills were also of some quality for I had gone to wait for him on the roof. Steve did not quibble with my diagnosis and half an hour later I was heading for hospital in Aberdeen – my first psychiatric hospital in twenty years.

Although I did not expect to crack up so spectacularly I knew that I was in some sort of trouble. A severe knock back months previously had not helped. During my successful period in the voluntary sector I became less sure that my retirement from the world of paid work had been the right move. I confidently applied for a job as a day-care officer in the adult training centre where I had been doing (I thought) great things as a volunteer. My application got nowhere; the reason it got nowhere was a shock when I discovered the truth. I was not viewed as a gifted, competent and successful volunteer who was professionally qualified to do the job and who could do it standing on his head. I was viewed as a manic-depressive – as a centre-user.

Years on I can thank them for sending me away. It would certainly have been another damaging failure but the message was hard to take at the time; it really was all over. I felt humiliated, wronged, stupid, discarded and middle-aged. I fancy that a combination of middle-age crisis, male menopause and mania sent me on to the cottage roof – where else would you go with those three?

After a two-month lie up in hospital there was no new master plan to get me through the rest of my life. Everything had gone, including my social life.

In April 1996, although not a happy man and not sure about the effect that lithium carbonate was having on me, but at least depression free, in an act of desperation I looked out my mouldy collection of camping gear and set off for the hills. A risky undertaking at that time of year for an unfit fifty-year-old. I had not muddied a hill-walking boot in twenty years but I tried to do all the right things. With a full pack on my back it was a gruelling, cold and wet five-day trek from Aboyne to Braemar via Birse, Glen Esk, Glen Clova, Jock's Road and Glen Callater but I made it despite a couple of navigational frights and some unexpected snow. I lost five pounds and was to lose more on the other five treks I made that year.

That summer was more like it: no committees, no bossing people around in rehearsal rooms, no pursuit of perfection, no trying to change the world and, for long periods of time, no me either. Just the small survival decisions you make all the time on a hard solo trek in the mountains with a dry tent and warm sleeping bag at the end of the day.

The only times I wished I had company were when there was something special to see; like the otter hunting for eels at my feet in the Spey and the new-sloughed yellow and black adder – a coiled, vibrant jewel against the brown April grasses below Loch Avon. But, then, if you had been there they would have been off; the otter, the adder and the eagles would have heard us gabbing a mile away.

September saw the last trek of the year, a lung- and ankle-buster with some desperately bad midgie moments – I have never hated another species so much. The walk started at the Corran Ferry near Fort William and ended at Lochaline on the Sound of Mull. From the Fishnish Ferry it was a bus ride to Tobermory to visit my friends at the Little Theatre on Mull. I cooked them black pudding and apples with sautéed potatoes but never noticed, even as I balanced their kitchen knives on my nose, that I was feeling far, far too good. Hopelessly restless, I left them a note and hightailed it out of Tobermory early the following morning and had to wait two years to see Alasdair's brilliant production of *Whisky Galore*.

I was in hypomania but not yet able to spot it. It was a sociable journey home via Oban, Glasgow and Dundee in which I became pals with several of my fellow passengers – with a mother and daughter on the Glasgow bus giving me an idea for a novel.

At home with my rucksack lying unpacked behind me I was writing again after two years. Hey, maybe 'not working' could be writing again! But after a non-stop week I ran out of plot. Two of the characters went into a short story writing competition whilst the baddies – Big Billy Flynn and Malkie Spooner – are still holding their breath at Chapter Five. Maybe they will show up in a play sometime – certainly not in the novel I do not have in me.

I could not repeat my mountaineering the following year. Bouts of overwhelming fatigue dogged me and needed investigation. I imagined myself laid out in some midgie-infested glen and the embarrassment of the flight out in a big yellow helicopter. But I did not have the same stomach for it either. A social disaster I had with the theatre group I had established in the village still gave me considerable pain. Too much had been invested in that social bucket and in the spring of 1997 everything seemed to have come to another end again. 'Not work' was not working out.

Gardening, when I was able, helped me through that fatigue-ridden summer. Gradually I eased into a version of myself I had not known for a long time. The care taken with my lawns, fish-pond and flower-beds was a search for perfection right enough, but not of the Legoland kind, only the healthy, common gardener's variety. I began to mourn less for the worlds I had lost although it still hurt when something reminded me of them.

The fatigue lifted the following spring. My 'not work' plans were that as soon as the snow melted in the hills I would be off to them again – maybe in a month, I thought. I knew not to plan my route yet though – I had learned that with this illness a month is a long time.

Did I get away as planned? I cannot recall whether I did or not but I have continued to trek through the Highland wilds where, despite the lighter and better gear I now have, plus my greater experience, I still get into terrible scrapes!

11

Sideways Through the Torphins HaLF-*edj* – Ambulance Journey

Being carted off in an ambulance with some life-threatening physical condition would count with most of us as being a major low point but one's thoughts, as I recall, are pretty straightforward. 'Oh shit' is about as complicated as they get. If, however, it is to a ward in a psychiatric hospital that you are bound, your thoughts are all over the place. On one of the occasions when I needed to be admitted to a mental hospital I tried to insist on travelling in myself on the bus. At the surgery I pointed out that I had got myself there in a bus but I had told them also of the minutes on the number 270 when I realized that I was dead after hanging myself half an hour ago in the byre. Doubts about this being some new and marvellous form of me sitting on the New Pitsligo bus crept in when, compliments of the school-kids on the back seats, a flicked wad of paper bounced off my head and landed on the seat in front. I turned to look at the youths and they looked at me. Whatever it was they saw in my eyes stopped their play for the rest of their journey.

I felt the flat slam of ambulance doors shutting me down even before it had been called. As loopy as I knew I was, I needed to travel the forty miles into Aberdeen with Stagecoach. There in dim, unhurried, upholstered privacy I could let what was happening again happen gently.

The despair felt on being led into a psychiatric ward-bound wagon is total. I feel worthless, humiliated and sick with dread at whatever new humiliations are to be faced at my destination, but communicating any of this to those around me is not possible.

So I see the jokes. Maybe it is pride. Maybe it is a response to the pressure of being the object of the exercise and wanting to make this embarrassing situation easy for everybody concerned. There is also the capacity our species has of being able to spot and enjoy the absurdities of our existence even when we are in the shit – especially when we are in the shit. Or am I just whistling a happy tune so that no one will know I'm afraid? Whatever the purpose of the mask, it is one of those masks that take you over: a mask you become, for I do not feel fraudulent; I feel better, enjoying my observations and nonsense.

'The trouble with ambulances is that unless you are longways you have to sit sideways. Even backways is better than sideways.' I announce.

Although captive, it has to be said that there are better audiences to be had than those in the back of your average asylum-bound van. My observation of the seating arrangements was weak but the nurse could have done more with it.

'We'll soon be there,' she says, implying that we will soon be there. We have barely started and have an hour's drive in front of us but we will soon be there already. The humiliations have started. In this wagon I am just an entry in the ambulance crew's log, something to be loaded and unloaded and for a nurse, a nuisance or a chance to get out of the ward for a change. Humour the patient if it talks but though it be physicist or fish-gutter, do not be interested.

My escorts do not even converse with one another for fear of sharing something with me. All they have to do for their crust this night is get me to the ward. In this company, it would be easy to drift into dead again.

So we stop farting about on quarter impulse power once we clear the village, do we? Or have we clearance for taking the Ellon wormhole today? Well, just mind that you canna go through a wormhole sidewise – they've had some right old messes wi' that in the past. Me to me, of course.

I'll ask Audrey if by 'soon' she expects us to be shifting into warp drive. Maybe even discuss the problems of 'soon' with her – no, I won't.

> 'Hello, Brian. I'm Audrey, and I will be your psychiatric nurse today. This is Alec the ambulance driver. Julia is a student nurse. Would it be all right if she comes with us to observe?'

> 'The more the merrier,' I said and we all laughed at what a card I was and how much fun it was all going to be.

Though we are not yet in warp drive, the village passes briskly across the clear glass strip above the ambulance sides: the church, the chipper, the war memorial, the park, the school, a figure or two and then back into the blackness of the countryside again.

I think of where I am going and up flash incidents that hurt all over again.

> 3am and from a dimmed ward corridor I am led into a tiny, white, fluorescent-lit room in which a 40 watt lamp would be enough, kind and sensible. The admitting doctor and nurse have been okay but now they are my torturers. They tell me to subtract seven from a hundred, then seven from ninety-three and so on down to whatever you get but at the best of times my mental arithmetic is non-existent.

Until now I have been holding myself together quite well, been putting up a fair enough show but now they are going to see how stupid I am. No reassuring smiles now, just two blank pairs of young female eyes examining me. My face burns. They must see my embarrassment and humiliation. Desperately I try to clear away the crap that tells me I can't do this. Concentrate, just concentrate. 'Sixty-four, fifty-five, forty-f…six, thirty…, Oh Jesus.' There is not a blink as I falter. Concentrate, concentrate. 'Thirty… I am going to burst.'

Once in a Fraserburgh tea room I was served by a woman who looked so much like somebody I had seen elsewhere that to be sure she was not actually that other person I asked her who she was.

'Are you your double or are you just you?'

'Yes,' she said, she was, 'definitely just me.'

She knew of her double because other people had remarked on the similarity which, crucially for my patter, included bright, friendly eyes; but she had never met the other person even though Fraserburgh is not all that big a place.

I explained how these things happened occasionally and that it could be that her double was actually herself in another parallel Fraserburgh universe and that there must have been a slip in the space-time continuum.

'Oh I hope no,' she frowned, 'I'm going on my holidays next week.'

Ignoring her attempts to take the piss I continued.

'This would explain why the two of you, or this one of the two of you, if you see what I mean, have never met, for you can never meet. If you did the two dimensions would

collapse but, some things being equal, you'll still be
buttering my roll and I'll still be speaking to you in the
other dimensions but not necessarily in this jacket.'

'Gee,' she said, 'and I thought it wis just that this wifie
looked like me. Y'ken, maist folk come in here and just
speak about the wither.'

I could use her right now in this ambulance. In a tea room you can
make friends and get the biggest slice of gateau with patter like that.
Try that trekky stuff as an ambulance head-case and all that the likes
of Audrey will want to do is go faster.

> We are in the interview room for the second time that day.
> Earlier, the senior nurse who took me inside started to give
> me a bollocking for upsetting an assistant nurse – a nurse I
> quite liked. She was in the room too – looked upset. Had I
> really behaved that badly? Surely not. I remember the
> incident in which he says I behaved badly. Sure I was
> irritable but not abusive or anything. She gave no hint at the
> time of being upset. I do not understand what is going on. I
> feel my anger rise and walk out. Now, after I complain to
> the ward manager, we have been brought together so that
> the senior nurse can hiss out an apology. Then it was as if
> nothing had happened: the nurse I upset as bouncy and
> friendly as ever; he as cold as ever. But some meaningless
> thing happened leaving me confused and insecure. I don't
> want nurses being made to apologize to me. I want them to
> like me.

The ambulance overtakes the Aberdeen bus, my bus. A bright strip of
saloon lights, the driver's dark cab, its headlights disappearing
behind us then nothing. Will these nurses still be on that ward?

> In the afternoon medication queue a nurse threatens a
> young elated patient with having his medication

administered by injection instead of by the usual pill if he does not sit down and shut up.

I suppose that an Ei-Varp inbuild would be too much to expect in this pile. That would have us at the funny farm front door or in the men's toilets if you wanted, in *N.O.* time; from here, say about... oh...twelve minutes ago. Not the most direct of routes right enough: via the Lkocerian Cluster and through the Torphins HaLF-*edj* but, though there's probably a price to pay for it (in terms of matter shift – although nothing's ever been proven), at least you're comfortable sideways in an Ei-varp. In fact in a Ei-varp you know all about it if you are not sideways. Will that nurse still be there? I hope no. They say that ECT used to be used as a punishment. I believe it.

Strapped in side-saddlewise we continue to make our way through the black countryside: patient, nurse, student nurse, unseen ambulanceman driving, ambulanceman in the back. Like bottles in a crate we sway in unison to the Transit's impulse drive, i.e. the driver's erratic foot on the accelerator.

If you are not lying longways in an ambulance you look down at the shoes of the people opposite then up at the roof then after a look at the van's medical kit and bits and pieces it's back to the shoes across the way again but sooner or later, if you are me, something has to give; and so, although I should know better with this company, on sideways being I'm at it again.

'A bed in a sleeper carriage on a train is the worst kind of sideways: being pulled sideways at the same time as you are being pulled longways.'

'I've never thought about it like that,' says Audrey.

Encouraging.

'Well you should. I mean, on which side do you put your head? Next to where it is a hundred miles an hour or at your feet where folk walk along the corridor?'

'Do you like trains, Brian?'

So we try to speak about trains but nobody had been on the Kyle or Deeside lines or stood on the footplate of the *Union of South Africa* cooling down in its Markinch shed or had a grandfather who waved from the train he was driving, steaming for Inverness in his Black Five, or had anything at all to say about trains and so that was the end of that.

> The woman speaks to me like I am a piece of shit. Is it something about me that bothers her, does everything about being a psychiatrist bore her? Whatever is wrong, it makes me feel like a nothing. The nurse at her side is very still. Does she find all this unpleasant too or is it just all in my imagination? Am I going paranoid again?

I should have left that room. I will if anything like it happens this time. If anybody speaks to me like that psychiatrist again, I really will walk out – no subtracting tests either. I'll refuse it. But then they'll say I'm being unco-operative – not helping them to help me. I might be nuts and have just come in from The Pits, but that's no excuse.

> The psychiatric hospital's x-ray day is a cattle mart. I cannot stand it any more and get up and walk out. Outside, in the sun, a nurse comes after me. 'Mr Adams, come back here right now!' I did the same again the following month.

Another village slips by: another chipper, the police station, the pub where at the Saturday karaoke my *Strangers in the Night* went down well. Under the garage lights people fill up their tanks. The screen goes black again.

It is hard to be the life and soul in the back of an ambulance when everybody is waiting for you to crack up.

So crack up then.

An appalling fantasy occurs to me, in which I take control. The wee student nurse in the corner is to be kicked out of the ambulance at the next lay-by.

> *'Get that kid out of my psychosis. I take back my permission for her to be here on the grounds that she has not brought anything along for the raffle.'*

'Hello, Brian. I'm Audrey, and I will be your psychiatric nurse today. This is Alec the ambulance driver. Julia is a student nurse. Would you mind if she comes with us?'

> *'Yes I do. Bugger off, Julia.'*

Julia might be about twelve and a half and looks about as happy observing me as a vampire in a health food shop. I decide to let her stay.

> 'This is your bed.' Somebody has been cleaning his comb and I look down at a greasy wad of grey hair in the dirty aluminum ashtray stamped 'Kensitas'. The nurse who has led me to my first bed in my first psychiatric hospital does not appear to notice this offence on my bedside locker. He leaves and the elderly patient in the next bed comes up and asks if I have been drinking too much. Is that, he wants to know, why I am here?

Once I shared an inbound ambulance with an old man who had had a heart attack. I would have changed illnesses with him in a second. I watched him from Julia's corner.

> 'You go to the funny farm with my good ticker and I'll go to the infirmary with your ropey one where I will lie back and let them do this and that, and where I will be sent 'Get Well Soon' cards, fruit and flowers and be home in a few weeks with instructions on how to live the rest of my life.'

But he would never have agreed and we went our different ways at Aberdeen. A year later I sang for him and his sheltered housing pals at a Burns Supper. He looked fine.

I drove an ambulance myself for a short period during the ambulance strike of 1974. I was a convinced trade unionist but almost two years previously an ambulance team had arrived at my flat with a bottle of oxygen when it seemed that I was on my last sip of the natural stuff as I lay on my living room floor. 'Oh shit,' I could not say. 'I thought you boys were never going to get here,' was another I could only mouth. I imagined somebody in that fix and nobody coming to help and so, like the neep I was, I responded to the call for volunteer ambulance drivers or, if you were a striking ambulance crew, bastard scabs!

And that is how I found myself driving past pickets of demented ambulance drivers. A few times I spotted one of the guys who had saved my life with his oxygen and his patter. Now he was tearing off my left wing mirror and shouting into the cab that I was a dead man!

Here was more material better kept to myself although I realized that the modern paramedic/action-man version sitting opposite me, would have been about two at the time of the strike. Another good reason for not bothering him was that he, star of *Casualty, Blues and Twos, 999* and a dozen other TV documentaries, had nodded off into a sound sleep. So much for my patter.

I feel the bend where Sonia was killed and then the pause at the junction at the top of the hill. From the bypass we see the lights of Ellon half a mile away. We are more than halfway there.

Cue Audrey: 'It won't be long now,' said Audrey.

12

Pantiled Peep Show – Modern Psychiatric Hospital Building

At the other side of the road from the bakery where I worked for five years as an apprentice baker stood the high granite walls of a psychiatric hospital. Like the rest of the city I did not wonder too much about what went on behind these walls which was probably the intention. Some of the walls have been demolished now to show off a large and glamorous newcomer. To the collection of granite buildings, the unhappiest of which were quite correctly hidden from view, the new, thirty-million pound building takes pride of place.

The thing is one large building but if you really try hard it can seem like a group of separate buildings. Here a two-storey gable-end, there a long, low bungalow, this bit round, that bit square, up there a tower, down here a courtyard and around it all the landscaping: car parks and the usual grass carpet fitted to the spits, nooks and crannies formed by this attempt at a village. Dreary shrubs catch the wind-blown litter but otherwise do nothing but exist whilst here and there inexplicable rectangular slabs of rough-hewn granite are set recumbent in the grass like ancient gravestones. Perhaps the stones were planted for us to puzzle over; I look and see and enjoy for a moment how the natural grey of the stone contrasts with the man-made brickwork which overlooks them. Maybe that's it, but could the 'graves' be intended to suggest an ancient site, another contrast to consider: the old and new, who knows? The external walls of the building are cream in colour and decorated with pleasing detail but, up top, are the pantiles – oh yes and oh dear, the red pantiles. If you were thinking for a second that this really was a group of separate buildings, the roof is a bit of a giveaway for every inch of it is clarted* with identical pantiles: same colour, same shade, same size, same style. Nobody thinks this place looks like a collection of buildings and I would guess that nobody cares very much.

Inside it is a hamster's play station of tunnels, twists and turns, steps, dips, flyovers, dog-legs, glass runs, nooks and crannies – the building's users paying the price for this rambling conceit. The main tunnel, a wide arcade-like carpeted street, leads you past the elaborate but dark entrances to the hospital's various branches: Occupational Therapy, Physiotherapy, etc.

Halfway along the main tunnel thick, complex odours herald the hospital kitchen approaches: olfactory offences entirely appropriate to the visual ugliness around in the obscure art forms in ceramics and steel that stud the tunnel walls. More arty puzzles hang from the roof. Puzzles as in 'What the hell is that?'

Entering the acute wards themselves is much less artistically challenging. In one of them the doors open into an airy lounge whilst in the others the newcomer steps into another long, windowless tunnel.

Soon the newly admitted patient finds out how the ward works. He sees that the showers and toilets located off each of the five-bedded rooms are fine but, bemused by the tiny wash-hand bowl and the treacherous face-splitting fixtures that tell you that these are strictly for hands only, he goes looking for the room with the sinks. Y'know, where you can splash around a bit, get in behind your ears and, crucially for the likes of me, where you can wet shave.

---

*   Daubed or besmeared (Scottish)

A patient showed me where it was, the one and only basin suitable for face washing in the entire ward. It is in the bathroom. Its gadgetry suggests that it is intended for hair washing but it does fine.

Following other sorties into your new environment you understand why you keep hitting the ward's open doors as you pass through them. This is due to the official practice of keeping the narrow extension part of the doors permanently open and the wide door proper, closed. You could ignore this slim but obvious route and still push open the main door but you do not and in no time even the bulkiest of patients gets the measure of these gaps in the wall. In a manoeuvre reminiscent of The Military Two Step – right step, turn, left foot following through – everybody learns to glide obliquely through the ward's doors. Try closing these doors in the rooms for a bit of seclusion and the first surprised nurse who comes across this odd thing, i.e. a closed door, will painstakingly undo the extension's catches and return the access to its proper, two-foot-wide, psychiatric-ward state.

If you are touchy like me, being made to go through doors sideways is a minor humiliation but, fortunately, like much that one encounters as a powerless patient in a large and complex institution, it is also too funny to want to plot any kind of protest.

But you are tired. You have been taken here from whatever your nightmare was and have not slept for a while. You lie back on your bed and then take in the noise – a constant rumble of air being blown through a black metal vent in the roof. Passengers on the old Stornoway ferry took in less noise than patients do from the air-conditioning system in these wards. Some fortunate souls do not appear to notice it at all, but coming from the rural silence I live in, I notice it all right.

That rumble can become an insistent roar, as I was to discover when stuck under it for three solid days with flu. In fevered desperation I tried to stuff its slats with rolls of newspaper. I thought I had done well until a second after plugging the last slat: in an explosion of newsprint all hell broke loose above me and there was a moment when I feared that *The Times* was going to pulp me to a newsworthy death. Thankfully, in what is a wonderful moment, the system is switched off at night.

The acute wards have a number of single rooms. During one admission I would have given a lot to have the quiet and privacy of one. The six-person room I shared was as seedy as any I have experienced. The tumble dryers in the patients' laundry room had permanently packed in and so washing lay draped over the heaters in the rooms and on the airers provided. The basic cleaning arrangements appeared to have broken down and the bed areas of two of the patients opposite looked like grenades had hit them.

This is not how I live and there came a time when living in this room was becoming unbearable. I asked a nurse to find out if I really needed to stay in hospital any longer. A young doctor came to see me.

Doctor I hear that you are a bit unhappy.

Me Yes, I'm not so ill as I was and I was wondering if I really needed to stay any longer.

Doctor We'd like you to stay a bit longer so that we can monitor the effect of your medication.

Me My GP can do that. I've had lithium before.

Doctor Well, we would still like a few more days with you here. If something could happen to make it possible for you to stay what would it be?

Me A room to myself.

Doctor I'm afraid that there are none available and we couldn't put someone out of theirs to give you one.

Me Of course not. I haven't asked for a single room because I knew I wouldn't get one. I wouldn't want somebody kicked out just to suit me. I just answered your question.

Doctor   Sure. Is there nothing else that would help; have you gone swimming?

Me   No. In this day and age do you not think it is ridiculous to build a new hospital with so few single rooms? It's just about cost.

Doctor   Well, I think it's about problems to do with the observation of patients too. Have you been going to aerobics?

Me   No. I did intend to go to the pictures today.

Doctor   What's on?

Me   *Contact.*

Doctor   Okay, then. Why don't you still go to the pictures? Give it another night and we'll meet for another chat the same time tomorrow. How about that?

The chat with the junior doctor kept me there another night but I slipped out the following morning after the switching on of the air-conditioning in the morning. I had been grateful to be admitted and although I had considerable fears about going home, I was just too unhappy in the place and too depressed to talk about it any more.

Aspects of the building tell us that the newest of psychiatric hospital planners still build to Victorian standards of patient privacy practices. Not even soldiers are kept in barracks these days.

Perhaps one day the NHS will build psychiatric hospitals in which all patients who can be in single rooms will have them. We will look back on six-bedded rooms and view them with the same mixture of horror and amusement with which (I hope) we all view the large multi-bed wards I experienced twenty years ago.

For whom did the health authority design this building? For its users within or an audience without? Are the red roofs and its public art something to dazzle the citizens with as they roar past on the road outside; a statement to the public about mental health care as delivered by their friendly local NHS Trust? 'Hey, everybody, look at our swanky new mental hospital, look at all the arty distance we have travelled from the bad old asylum days.' Then the public, after its positive encounter with psychiatric stanes and plaster, will go home with its crummy attitudes towards mental illness starting to change which would be a very wonderful thing indeed.

So much for the public, what about staff and patients? The building was surely built for them, right? Well, my experience of a hospital with no sinks, noisy vents and no privacy tells me that this pile was not built for patients. Patients evaluate a hospital from inside, not out. The hi-spec glam was not created for patients.

My information is that nursing staff have disliked being presented with this rambling conceit as much as people like me. Not, I would add, with any noticeable effect on their professionalism. The best of the nurses I know well from my years of admissions could give good nursing care in an air-raid shelter.

So how did this mess come about? I suppose that the building might simply have been the work of managers in idealistic-mode and that we are simply looking at a corporate cock-up. Perhaps it is more unpleasant than that and naturally I am drawn to a more sinister kind of idiocy. I fancy that the building was designed for its designers.

Prestige is everything in this NHS pile. I see a self-indulgent brief with little else in mind but a creation to project the image that the managers have of themselves – to themselves. The old walls did not come down to let patient's look out or to let a stigmatizing public peek in. This is management speaking and showing off to itself; propagandists consuming their own propaganda.

In my dictatorship I would make managers inhabit their hospitals for a time: NHS executives, hospital trust convenors, managers, nurses, doctors, architects. After sharing a room with four of the likes of me for a week I feel that their view of their hospital might change a tad.

13

Psychos! – Acute Psychiatric Ward

Alex[*] is a tall, quiet person of about thirty. He never initiates a conversation but when he does he surprises by speaking up boldly and without any apparent shyness. He only leaves his bedside to go for meals and to make cups of coffee which he brings back to the room to drink standing up. Each cup lasts about fifteen minutes so this is a lot of coffee in a day. No television or mixing with other patients, no radio, tapes, reading or walks; just his meals, non-stop coffees and trousers off for bed at night.

Billy is difficult to age but I guess him to be about twenty. Pale, short and lightweight, the first thing you notice is the raw flesh below his eyes as a result of him picking out the maggots that he sees and feels there. He is the most obviously disturbed person in the ward. Often in the evening he asks me to go with him to one of the small grocery shops near the hospital for sweets. I always do but he will not go to the shop I prefer on a different street because he is afraid of that street's evil powers. A tall factory tower that overlooks the street is at the core of the malevolence and crossing the main road, where we come within sight of it, he becomes very quiet. Mostly, though, Billy is in bed, not surfacing until three or four in the afternoon even though every morning at ten his *Star Trek* alarm clock

[*] The names of the people in this chapter are false.

warns us that the Enterprise is in great danger. But the Klingons can have the hospital and the whole Federation fleet on a plate for all that Billy cares. He sleeps about fifteen hours a day: through breakfast, lunch, intra-muscular injections, alien attacks and the noises of the day. No amount of exhortations from the nursing staff stir him. To be brought early out of the place he prefers to be he would have to be dragged out, but fortunately the staff are not into that. We celebrated his birthday with a cake baked by a nurse which he passed around.

Colin is eighteen and in trouble with drugs, cannabis in particular. He has used it since he was a schoolkid and it is now giving him serious problems. He is a cheery, intelligent and decent lad. He is a keen on the outdoors, loves to chat, has a great sense of humour and fancies his chances with a young female patient. He is a solid, intelligent lad; I can see why his firm would want to give him every chance to hold on to his apprenticeship. He goes home for the weekend leaving his bed and surrounding area a tip.

Donald is a farmer. A slight figure of about sixty, they are treating his depression with a course of ECT. His wife travels in every day bringing, amongst other things, changes of beige jerseys but otherwise she is of no good to him. After one afternoon visit left him in tears, he was watched closely for the rest of the day. She had told him to stop his nonsense and come home to get on with running the farm. The staff took it in shifts to watch him: sitting at the back of the lounge when he watched telly and in the corridor outside our room with a magazine when he dozed. The following day he was fine. The ECT he gets seems to be helping.

Eric is in his twenties. He was a nurse until he became ill. His packed bed area tells of someone who has been in hospital for a while: guitar and boxes of stuff under the bed, lots of family photographs, his children's drawings, the bedside cabinet stacked with fruit, drinks, sweets, a paint-by-numbers kit. He is unsmiling, mild-mannered and, like Alex, never initiates conversation. His wife has left him and his nursing career may be over too. Eric told me to play his guitar any time I wanted too (he cannot play himself). He is far too generous and a young manic-depressive from another room is taking fags and money off him. Donald reported it to a nurse but it is still going on.

Fiona and I often meet up in the lounge and dining area. She suffers from terrible depressions. She is under pressure from her husband to leave hospital but her psychiatrist wants her to stay for a good while yet. 'Mummy' her young daughter cries, running into the lounge and burrowing, marsupial-like, into her mother's skirt. Fiona is in her thirties. We get on and walk in the park at least once a day, usually in the evening. Once, on telling the ward office that we were going out, a nurse embarrassed us by making a suggestive remark. This is not Fiona's first stay here. Once she showed me the 'secret garden' tucked away in a disused corner of the hospital grounds where on a previous admission she lay in the snow and wept.

Gale is in her thirties. She is shy, very attractive, but smiles all the time. She sometimes comes out with Fiona and me and joins in a bit with the conversation but gives away nothing about her illness. Like most of the group that meets around the television she watches every soap there is. She wants Fiona and me to go to aerobics down at the physiotherapy department with her. She complains about the untidiness in her room too.

Hugh is an architect. He pulled me into the 'Trivial Pursuit' circle on my first evening on the ward. His lithium was keeping him in his job until carelessness with it threatened disaster again. Like me, it takes Hugh a while before it clicks that something is wrong. On this occasion it took a running dive into the boating pond of a park before he would let his wife take him to the doctor. She was great fun too. I wish I had stayed in touch with them.

Ian is a baby. A real live crying baby who I sometimes hold and amuse with funny voices at mealtimes while his mother goes up to the food trolley. This baby-caring privilege is sought by others but mostly their timing and positioning is poor and so often this real thing to do is mine. Postnatal depression is the obvious guess as far as his mum's illness is concerned but it could be anything. Some babies are resident, some are brought in. These mums have lots of visitors and the babies crawling about the ward are great fun. I found one in the kitchen once. Sometimes the student nurses steal them away and the mothers, for whom the babies are brought in, do not get a look in.

Jim, a retired teacher, plunged suddenly into a rambling, confused old man. Daily we – his family and the other patients – watch him deteriorate further. Sometimes he becomes very agitated and unhappy and it is difficult for us to have him beside us. At other times he makes us smile when he wakes up from his chair and looks around with a huge grin. Although he sleeps most of the time, Ian's folk spend a lot of time in the lounge with him and so spend a lot of time with us. They chat away, watch the soaps and go 'Ah' along with everybody else at kittens in *Pet Rescue*. The wife tells us all about Ian; what a great chap he was and about the incident that upset him and made him like this. She is holding herself well but it is a burden on us patients. On top of what we have to experience with Ian we also have to experience her anguish. She asks that I make sure he watches *Songs of Praise* which this Sunday is to feature the church in which Ian is an Elder. She does not see that Ian is past knowing what a church is or what God is or even what she is. She knits as he sleeps in the chair next to her. Once, as she pulled at a ball of wool, she asked what was wrong with me which I thought was a bit off. Ian will not be condemned to a geriatric ward for the rest of his life until his psychiatrist is sure that this is a permanent condition. Fair enough, but it is very hard on some of us.

And this is who you might meet in an acute ward. Some of us certainly a bit odd but does the pejorative 'psychos' suit us?

If a television dramatist were to accurately depict us in a play about life in a modern psychiatric hospital, his efforts would not get past the first producer's yawn. Forget the television drama you have seen of us, in my experience acute psychiatric wards are not very exciting places. Sure I have seen unpleasant and sometimes disturbing incidents, but then I've observed that in medical wards too. There was the tackling (literally) by staff of a patient under section who refused his medication. I've listened to hours of desperate weeping in the next room and once there was a lad who if you said the wrong thing would sing through every Beatles number there was. And there was Mary, the shy, pale, delicate, long-haired girl transfixed by the voices that called to her from the ceiling. Nothing there to fill a 'psychos' script.

I tell you that the only 'mad' incident in my acute psychiatric ward experience was the flaming bin which was, of course, a crazy staff moment. That and the putting green antics certainly have comic mileage in them. I'd love to see that nursing outfit recreated on the telly but, plot-wise, this is about as much as I can come up with – about four minutes of telly.

The story I have is of the particular brand of ordinary life to be found within an acute ward, of how people in crisis with a variety of illnesses can form themselves (despite the system) naturally into a tolerant, therapeutic community which can feel like a family. Stays in psychiatric hospitals can be lengthy and so patients can get to know one another well. Real and lasting friendships can develop and, of course, so too does love. I never had such good luck.

I would not pretend that ward life is 'The Waltons' but little rituals become established like daily walks in the same company, 'Trivial Pursuit' after tea, toast-making at suppertime, a patient returning with the Saturday night takeaway orders. At bedtime a lassie in dressing gown and slippers might curl up in the chair next to you with her cocoa and laugh at your patter and at breakfast an older version, still in hair curlers, will see that the toast keeps coming for everybody. You fix her broken necklace. A lad offers you a loan of his CD player – you tell him to get some condoms if he really is going to be trying his luck with that girl in the next room.

And so the trust, the intimacies and the often unlikely friendships develop. Everyone's bare fact of suffering from a mental illness is out in the open in this safe, unprejudiced place and all that matters here is how people are: is he kind, is she approachable, is he decent, is she fun, is he feeling as lousy as me? Patients come and go, of course, but the group experience can be all the healthier for this fluidity; the constantly changing patient mix helping to keep the interactions fresh and inclusive.

Patients talk about feeling safe in hospital and however much dread I have felt on my way in and as difficult as I have found aspects of hospital to be, I have always felt this sense of security straight away. Most of the responsibilities of life are removed from you here and in some ways it is like being a child again but, moving right along from some 'O level' Freudian stuff that occurs in which the staff play Mother and Father, I ask is there anything in the society I have described that you could dramatize without sending the telly nation to sleep? Anything you could entitle *Psychos*? I do not think so.

Just as Hollywood tells us of a West populated with handsome cavalry captains, ruthless cattle barons and sexy saloon girls (to name just John Wayne,, Jack Palance and Barbara Stanwick), British television's treatments of the psychiatric subject would have its audiences believe that psychiatric wards are populated by foul-mouthed, sex-addicted, long-haired raving, paranoid psychopaths and super-energized, super-gifted manic-depressives. All of them, of course, engaged in crucial conflicts and hilarious sub-plots and that…wait for it…is only the psychiatrists!

Storylines on the theme of the practitioners being in a worse state than those they practice upon is the dramatist's staple: police more crooked than the crooks, clergy as the anti-Christ, cannibalistic psychiatrists.

They – the doctors, nurses, police officers, prison warders, vets, fire-fighters and the rest of TV drama's stock in trade – may or may not like how they are portrayed on the box and will know whether they are harmed by it or not. What I know is that everybody is harmed by show biz when it tells society that mental hospitals are full of crazies and crazy goings-on and that you can laugh all you want.

When they put up the various clichés like the 'Jesus Christ Patient' and the 'Napoleon Patient' etc., you are made to laugh at the lives spoiled by the devastating mental illness which causes such delusions. So go on and laugh, why don't you, at the nineteen-year-old transfixed by the voices in the ceiling, hoot at her lost hopes for a career in teaching and double up at Billy, the lobsterman no more, picking his face raw.

And when they shock you with their portrayals of chaotic, hellish, psychiatric hospitals where the language in the doctors' room is worse than an army barracks and where, to off-stage shrieks and wails, patients fish for trout in the hospital lounge and have wild sex in the corridors, you take in a lie which is going to devastate you if mental illness ever visits your world. Imagine you or any of your family having to go into a place like that! The perception of an acute ward which the entertainment industry peddled you will be one of the reasons why you will feel such dread and refuse to be admitted.

The people who produce these grotesque portrayals of mental illness are the same people who centuries ago charged the public a fee to come into the asylums and be entertained by the demented lunatics. Then, as now, mental illness was exploited at the expense of a defenceless group of people whose suffering was not in any way of their own making and whose predicament was made far worse than it needed to be.

With television giving you the best seat in the madhouse, institutionalized stigmatization of mental illness is alive and well. In these, so-called, enlightened times primitive fears and social stigma are reinforced by the most sophisticated and powerful medium on earth. I tell you, society will never cure itself of its fear of psychiatric illness.

14

Tack Short of a Fitted Carpet – Synonyms

Away wi't, away with the fairies, bam, bampot, bananas, basket-case, batty, bats in the belfrey, bedlamite, bipolar, bonkers, book short of a library, candidate for Bedlam, catatonic, certifiable, clinically depressed, confused, crackbrain, crackpot, cracked, crackers, crank, cranky, crazy, cuckoo, darkened, depressive, demented, 'depryved of the use of their reasone', deranged, disordered, dipstick, disturbed, doolally, eccentric, emotionally disturbed, feeble-minded, few tacks short of a fitted carpet (made that one up myself – a friend came up with: 'husky short of a sledge team'), fruit cake, fruit loop, gaga, head-case, hypochondriac, hysteric, insane, kook, loco, lost his marbles, loon, loony, loony tunes, loopy, lost his reason, lunatic, mad, mad as a hatter, maladjusted, manic madman, maniac, megalomaniac, melancholic, mental, mentally abnormal, mental case, mentally disordered, mentally disturbed, mentally afflicted, mentally sick, meshuggenah, neuropath, neurotic, not in his right mind, non compos mentis, not all there, not the full shilling, not with us, nut ball, nuts, nutty, nutter, odd, oddball, obsessive, of unsound mind, off his chump, off his rocker, off his head, out of his mind, paranoid, personality disorder, phobic, psycho, psychopath, psychopathic personality, psychotic, queer in the head, rabid, raving, raving lunatic, round the bend, round the twist, scattered, sectionable, screwball, screwy, screw loose, schizo, schizoid, schizophrenic, sick, slice short of a sandwich, slowcoach, sociopath, soft, the blues, Tom o' Bedlam, toup, unbalanced, unhinged, unstable, wandered.

15

The Last Time I Saw Linda – Electroconvulsive Therapy

How is it done? Under a general anaesthetic electrodes are placed on the patient's head and an electrical current is passed through the brain producing a convulsion.

How does it work? I read that it is still not fully understood. It is said that the clue to its discovery was that it was noticed that some epilepsy sufferers felt their mood lighten after a fit.

In the early days Psychiatrist Number One sent me along to a general hospital for about half a dozen hits of ECT. I think they were given at the rate of twice a week. My failure to recall the exact details is more likely to be a consequence of the twenty-odd years that have passed since the treatment rather than the effect that it notoriously has on the memory.

Some of it was, though, a hoot. While lying in a bed on the hospital's day ward waiting to be given my first shot of ECT, I found that I must have dozed off for a moment and woke up to find Nurse Goodsir at my bedside. I knew her. We had gone out together a bit. I think her first name was Linda.

Nothing developed between us but, anyway, there she was again. It was a nice surprise and I felt really happy to see her. Instantly I was wide-awake.

'Hi, Brian.'

'Hi, Linda. You work here as well do you?'

'Aye, sometimes.'

[*There was something odd about how she was looking at me, like she was studying me.*]

'I'm here to get ECT.'

'You've had your treatment,' she said. 'Would you like a cup of tea?'

And that's the kind of effect on the memory that ECT can have. It was to be months before I could remember anything about the day prior to the giving of the general anaesthetic. All of it had been wiped: rising, bathing, bussing it in to the hospital, arriving at the ward, being wheeled in for the treatment. I knew what I was in the hospital for but the how and when was a blank.

In time my recollection of all of the day's events was to return: from feeding my tropical fish before I left the flat to the anaesthetist's jab. One day I just noticed that it was all there, without really noticing when – if you see what I mean.

In the day ward I was stripped of my seventies tulip-lapelled, flared suit and laid out in timeless hospital pyjamas.

'Have you eaten anything since last night?' asked the nurse [*not Nurse Goodsir*].

'No.'

'Is there no one here with you?'

'No.'

'You're an awful man. The letter told you to bring someone with you. You're supposed to have someone with you.'

[*I had nobody to come with me.*]

'It's okay, we'll keep you a while before we let you go home.'

I was wheeled into a small treatment room where two guys in black suits were waiting. Nobody spoke. One of them had a needle and...whoops, I must have dozed off for a moment. What a nice surprise it was to see Linda.

'Hi, Brian.'

'Hi, Linda. You work here as well do you?'

'Aye, sometimes.'

'I'm here to get ECT.'

'You've had your treatment. Would you like a cup of tea?'

Then I noticed the headache. A bad headache but a new kind of headache; the kind that tells you that something has been done to your brain – hopefully, just Electroconvulsive Therapy.

The tea afterwards always came with a plain digestive biscuit which, having fasted for the ECT and not having eaten since teatime the day before, was very welcome. I still cannot look at a digestive biscuit without 'ECT' flashing up; possibly because as far as my reality on the ECT afternoons was concerned, eating one in a state of hunger that I could not explain was the first act of the day. I did not know that I had not eaten since the day before. The day had been wiped; the hospital could have been making me work all morning in the laundry for all I knew.

Or treating me twice a week with digestive biscuit therapy. It is said that the whole palaver involved in administering ECT contains a strong placebo effect. There was tell of a hospital with a faulty machine which though not delivering a charge was still getting good results. Whether fact or urban myth, it is easy to understand how a patient entering positively into the ECT process/ritual might not need the actual shock to derive benefit from it. So perhaps a believer is likely to benefit more from a genuine course of ECT than the unbeliever who has had to be dragged into it. By 'dragged' I am, of course, in these modern times, speaking metaphorically for ECT history/mythology also has it that in the bad old days the treatment was sometimes used as a form of punishment.

Somebody just had to measure the placebo effect in ECT though, hadn't they? In a more credible version of the faulty ECT machine story, a study actually was undertaken in which some patients were given the full ritual: starvation, pyjamas, reassurance, anaesthesia and, no doubt, a cup of tea and a digestive biscuit afterwards. The full ritual but, deliberately, not the Full Monty. Instead of giving one group their one hundred volts, the doctor had a fag. Some patients were reported to have done quite well on the joke version but most did not see it at all and stayed depressed. Presumably, for the gag to work, none of the patients (suffering from severe depression, let us remind ourselves) involved in the study were told by their psychopathic psychiatrists that they were participating in such crucial medical research.

For years afterwards I blamed ECT for my bad memory and wished that I had never agreed to it. I do seem to remember that it did me some good but how long the effects lasted and just how much good it did is either lost to memory or unmemorable. Either way I just can't remember.

Quarter of a century on and I would have ECT again if it was suggested (and assured that I was not part of a study). The attraction is being zapped out of The Pits in an electric burst instead of waiting a month for an anti-depressant and its side effects to kick in or not kick in although I do not think that this is how ECT is used.

But the nervousness around this treatment never goes away. I saw the term 'ECT survivors' being used on the Internet in relation to people who wish now that they had not taken it.

Linda never appeared again after that first time and I never saw her again. She was awfully bonny – jet black hair. She will be into her fifties now too. I'm pretty sure now that her first name was Linda.

16

Sweet Violets – The Psychotherapist

In the early, pre-diagnosis eighties talking my problem out with a psychotherapist seemed like the answer to my problems. My doctor at the time was happy to set it up. He warned me that the therapist might be a 'bit rude'.

And yes, she was something that was unpleasant and so too was everything else about the encounter: in a dour room off a dour corridor in the most Eastern European looking of the hospital's collection of asylum buildings, I experienced my first and last encounter with psychotherapy. Basically, the sessions consisted of me trying to think of important things to say while my therapist helped by staring expressionlessly at the floor somewhere – a blank, empty thing that communicated by repeating everything I said.

This was medicine before anaesthesia and penicillin; a barium enema was a wild week in Las Vegas compared to this; I have gifted my body for dissection – I know already what it is going to feel like. Am I making myself clear? I really did not enjoy psychotherapy.

What would it have taken to dent that psychotherapy persona she created? A fire next-door maybe? I doubt it.

Patient	[*Telling Tommy Cooper jokes.*] 'Lie on the couch,' said the therapist to the patient. 'What for?' asked the patient. 'I need to sweep the floor,' said the therapist.
Therapist	What I'm hearing from you today is that sweeping the floor was important to the therapist.
Patient	[*Sniffing the air.*] I smell smoke!
Therapist	You seem to smell smoke today.
Patient	Yes, I have a good sense of smell and I do smell smoke.
Therapist	You seem to be very certain about the smoke.
Patient	Look, the hospital is on fire. I'm getting out of here.

[*Sounds of fire alarms, people screaming, breaking glass, fire engines, etc. coming from outside.*]

Therapist	I'm picking up lots of special effects from you today.

But there was never a fire and after the half hour-long sessions I would drive the forty miles home to Peterhead wondering what she, or I, had been getting at.

Once or twice I was late for the sessions and on one occasion forgot about it altogether. Desperately embarrassed, I tried to apologize the following week. Back bounced my apologies ('You say you are sorry' etc.) but this time the non-response contained something: a suggestion, something she wanted me to understand. Eventually, I saw it: my lateness was not caused by incompetence or by accident, it was a subconscious expression of my dislike or my fears or my resistance or something not good towards the therapy process.

Well, at that time in my life I was living at a hundred miles an hour and was late for everything – meetings, parties, dates, ferries, tides. I was chronically unreliable for everything but had not recognized the state I was in. Instead I believed her suggestion that I was resisting the therapeutic process.

It seemed that my illness, these crazy mood swings, was self-inflicted also. 'Whatever is wrong it must be something pretty dark and deep,' I thought. 'Maybe I don't want to uncover it. Maybe I don't really want to get better at all. Aye, that's it – I need to be depressed one week and swinging from the chandeliers the next; it's some kind of escape tactic I have developed. What do I need to escape from? There must be something I am escaping from.' And back to the days of head-banging I would go.

Is it possible that my therapist was just as pissed off with my lateness as any doctor, dentist, chiropodist, tattooist would have a right to be and that instead of forgiving me or giving me a straightforward bollocking, she climbed into my head with her annoyance?

I came to hate that miserable room and to dislike the woman who showed more regard for the cracks in the asylum's linoleum than me. If she knew of the pain and confusion which was my life at the time and of how hard I wanted the therapy to bring me an answer, there was nothing to show it.

Then there was the day I entered that room and noticed that she had pinned a small flower to her cardigan, a violet. It was a mistake. Suddenly I saw the human being, the person. I saw her in the early morning sunshine stooping to pick the flower and threading the delicate stalk carefully through the close weave of her patterned Fair Isle cardigan; decorating herself, being herself.

My eyes moved from her face to the violet then back to the face again. The face, as ever, angled downwards and to the side.

But she couldn't fool me anymore. The wall she pretended to be was part of the act. Before it had disturbed me but now, after seeing that sweet, sexy, moment with the violet, the whole thing seemed a silly, pointless, unnatural game between two people; a game that was achieving nothing.

I like my people engaging with me as if we were members of the same species; looking at me, if not in the eye, at least in my direction. Returning smiles is good too – even if that can be a game also. What kind of trade was this for a human being to ply and what, I wondered, did it cost her to keep it up?

'You seem to find it difficult to begin today.'

The sequel, half an hour later, might have come out of a movie script. It was a bonny spring day and after the session I went to think about all this daftness in the park adjacent to the hospital. There, about fifty yards off, not twisted in her chair, was the slim figure of the psychotherapist.

I sat on a bench and watched her take in the sunshine that cut through the still bare sycamores as she strolled, coatless, through the park. She looked thoughtful and unhappy. Under her arm was my file. She passed a bed of violets.

Was this what she did to keep herself from cracking up after half an hour with folk like me – take her time back through the park?

She went through the gate at the top end of the park and it was to be the last I ever saw of her. Maybe she was none of the things she looked like in the park but I was. That night I wrote a letter to her, withdrawing from the psychotherapy. She sent a kind letter back saying that she understood.

17

Sweating it Out with the Professionals – Doctors and Nurses

Psychiatrists

My head-case has been on the desks of seven psychiatrists. If the first had any good ideas he kept them to himself. The second diagnosed 'immature'. The third did mention mood swings and prescribed lithium carbonate but the words 'manic depression' never entered the conversation. The fourth was more like it: actually saying the words and strongly fancying them. At the one and only consultation with the fifth psychiatrist she read my notes as I spoke and then asked the observing student in the corner what he thought. He looked about as delighted with the lady as me.

'Yes, it certainly could be manic depression. It could quite easily be that. What do you think Donald?'

[*Donald nods and tries to look even smaller.*]

'But how much of it is manic depression and how much of it is you? That's the question isn't it, eh? How much of it is you?'

She retired from medicine soon after. I have it down as a close shave.

The diagnosis of manic depression was given to me at the first consultation I had with the consultant psychiatrist I was to see for ten years.

'I have gone through your notes…the pattern is clear…this is manic depression.'

Spoken twenty years after that first encounter with Psychiatrist Number One. I had moved about the country a bit but, c'mon, twenty years?

I had, however, started long before to home in myself on manic depression being the possible source of my troubles. The clues came in from here and there. The prescribing of lithium told me how at least one psychiatrist had been thinking when I bumped into a magazine article about the drug. There was a television programme about manic depression, which was all about me and, of course, there was the advantage of being able to observe myself swinging through life and doing all the things the various scraps of literature I came across said I should. But now it was official and being certain made all the difference. I could join the club, get used to the idea, recover from psychotherapy.

Some of the psychiatrists I have met along the way stand out. One always ended our meetings by taking a sample of blood for testing. She prepared for this by laying out the hypodermic syringe and the sample container neatly on the table for me to look forward to throughout the consultation.

'Brian, as your friend and as your doctor, you have my promise that you will get better.' So said a jovial young registrar. Everybody on the ward liked him. So did I but what a clown; I never saw him again. So much for psychiatrists as friends.

Finally, there was the seventies shrink who asked if I ever masturbated. What was he looking for: the first non-wanking twenty-five-year-old male in Scotland?

Psychiatric Nurses

One of the loneliest times of my life was spent in an acute ward when I had to take to my bed with flu. All I seemed to be to the few nursing staff who poked their heads around the bed screens was a source of amusement.

'Sweat it out, Brian. Ha, ha, ha.'

Shivering and soaked I lay under that rumbling air vent for four days. On the second night, a student nurse stopped by my bed and was delighted to do the sort of things that nurses do by fetching me fresh water, changing my sweat-soaked sheets and staying to chat a bit. But apart from her and whoever I bumped into when I went looking for paracetamol, I hardly saw a soul for three days.

Fortunately, being miserable enough with flu, I stopped taking lithium carbonate which had been making me feel nauseous prior to the infection. I say fortunately because, as I was to discover later, suspending lithium is advised in a patient with fever.

A thermometer and sphygmomanometer appeared at my bedside on the third afternoon and regular checks started to be made of my temperature and blood pressure. My guess is that a doctor recognized the significance of fever in relation to lithium therapy and ordered the monitoring – the exhortations to 'sweat it out' immediately stopped!

The best of the nursing staff I knew in the seventies were as competent as the best I have encountered in recent decades. Remembering everything from twenty-odd years ago is diffiult but I am sure that many of the nursing staff I remember from then were a different breed. Casual clothes have replaced the uniforms they wore then but if what I think I see now is typical, the profession has dumped some of its heart along with its whites. The psychiatric nurse as a therapy giver seems in danger of being lost to the psychiatric nurse as a mere observer, and note taker.

In a modern acute ward I spent time on there were times, thankfully only a few, when I experienced hours when the ward was filled with the despair of a patient weeping. Out goes your heart to them but this is major league misery – a job for nurses; at least they are in the right place to be in a state like that, you think. But then you pass their rooms and see that they are alone with their misery; nobody is attempting to comfort or distract them or just be with them. Such a patient, suffering from postnatal depression, told me how alone she felt on these occasions when we talked one day. I told her of how it had affected me and of the guilt I felt at not being able to do anything for her.

What else is psychiatric nursing for if it is not to be at the side of people in such low spirits? These incidents seemed to me to be akin to refusing morphine to a patient in severe physical pain. On these particular evening shifts in that ward, psychiatric nursing was for nothing more demanding than dishing out medications and writing up notes in the ward office. Cry out for dry pillows and a nurse would have given you all that you needed right away. Cry out for somebody to be with you and there was nothing doing.

To the visitor (only inhabiting the patients' lounge, of course) that ward at that time could seem like a pleasant enough place and mostly it was. Not, though, because of any informal efforts from nursing staff in the lounge; they seldom appeared there. A visitor once expressed to me how grateful she was that her husband was living in such a stimulating and friendly atmosphere – weren't the staff wonderful? I held my tongue. The woman had failed to notice during her visits just who were stimulating her husband and who were creating the atmosphere. The nursing staff dressed and washed her husband, fed him, took him to the toilet, gave him his pills and put him to bed but it was caring patients who put a comforting arm around him, listened to his ramblings and kept his behaviour acceptable when the staff turned him out into the lounge. Sometimes this was a most distressing and unfair burden on patients.

Whilst informal exchanges between staff and patients were nearly always friendly, I recall a ward where the lounge area was inhabited by patients only. I cannot ever recall nursing staff spending informal time with patients there. Even in the flaming bin dosshouse there were nurses who saw informal engagement with patients as part of their job.

I'll bet that the therapeutic, caring, listening image is the one that the public mostly holds of a psychiatric nurse. It is the one we are fed on in magazines and recruitment posters. But I have seen little to suggest that this is the truth about modern psychiatric nursing; little to show that informal time spent with patients is seen as an important part of the job – an opportunity to observe patients and practice a therapeutic role.

The importance of inter-patient bonding and patient society that I described in Chapter Thirteen is, I am sure, one of the ways in which some people can be helped to get better in hospital yet the interest taken in it by both medical and nursing staff appears to be nil. Indeed, I fear that it would come as news to them that outside their offices such a thing was in existence.

You do not need my 'A plus' to be a group worker. For example, it was kind of the nurse to make Billy a birthday cake but it was a therapeutic group activity opportunity lost. There was a lounge full of patients watching yet more television next to the kitchen where she made that cake. All she needed to do was be amongst them, pick her moment and it would have been patients who would have baked and decorated Billy's cake and maybe have put on a party too that would have made everybody feel good. Simple, powerful stuff but that evening, instead of a nurse/therapist enabling a positive experience for patients, all we had was a nurse baking a cake.

Some nurses indicate that they do not have time to sit with patients. Well some have time to bake a cake and there was the remarkable evening when two young nurses sat in the lounge for two hours one evening. Not to start a singsong; *Trainspotting* was on telly and they watched it straight through. Sometimes nurses have plenty of time.

However, despite modern psychiatric wards not being run exactly as prescribed by this expert, I have to say that I have nearly always left in a much better shape than the one I entered them in and the 'Thank You' cards that layer the ward's office walls tell of the system doing something right. The best of psychiatric nurses have my 'thank you' too. I hope that they know who they are

Students

Medical students need a supply of psychiatric patients to let them take a 'history' and I have always been pleased to participate. These sessions are surprisingly tiring – one a day is quite enough.

One came into my room the day after she had taken my history the day before. She had a copy of His Majesty's Theatre's monthly programme with her.

> *She*   Look, here's your play in the programme. I've been showing it to everybody and telling them that I took your history yesterday.

Inside the programme were the details and the date of my cancelled play. In the course of the history-taking I had told her about the cancellation – obviously I had not looked glum enough about it as I certainly did not need any graphic reminders of what should have been.

> *Me*   But...I told you...the show's been cancelled.
> *She*   I know, what a shame. But look, it's got a really good write-up in the programme.

Me	Well, of course it has.
She	[*More careful now – wondering if she had bumped into my big head or put a foot in my psychosis.*] Be…cause…it's such a good play?
Me	No. Because I wrote the write-up. [*Which I had.*]

One German medical student with blonde hair, blue eyes, flower-patterned frock, cricket pullover and black leather boots finished the taking of my history then broke new ground by asking if there was anything I wanted to know about her.

I was moved very much by these students. They were so fresh, clever and polite; it was a privilege to be of some help to them along the tough road they were on.

One mildly manic day it seemed only right that they should have my carcass as soon as possible. First chance I had I went down to the university and offered my body to the Department of Biomedical Sciences for dissection (once I had croaked, that is – I was not *that* elated).

I would love to be a fly on the wall in the anatomy room and watch a medical student peer inside my skull and find my healed, depressed fracture.

| *Student* | Wow! Look at the hole in this guy's skull! |
| *The Rest* | Jesus! |

In the course of conversation with two such students at a meeting of the Manic Depression Fellowship Aberdeen I told them that I had donated my body. They seemed quite moved. 'Thank you very much,' they said.

And, of course, you get student psychiatric nurses too. One, a lass from Rothienorman, 'observed' me on that body-donating outing. Sweetly she said that she thought she might donate her body too one day. Should I not wait a bit and think about it? It was unfair on her.

Her mission to 'observe' was not, I suspect, supposed to include anatomy labs and severe loopiness; all I had laid out for us in my time out of the ward was a visit to the art gallery. But the university was just along the road from the gallery and it had to be done then.

Another time out with a student nurse on board, I came back from town with the new white tuxedo I needed right away – £249, reduced to £179.

Back at the ward:

> 'I don't need to be in this bloody place. Do you like my new tux?'

I would love to see that student's notes. My sister took away the jacket and I did not see it for two years. I sold it to a friend. My body is still on offer to the university.

...and Mopped up by the System – Hospital Appearances

Dear Mr Adams,

Our investigations involving the Ward Manager and Nurse Manager are now complete and I write to advise you of the outcome.

The floors are cleaned on a regular daily basis as per the domestic's timetable. There can be from time to time the problem of patients' belongings being left lying around and the domestic being unable to move them, e.g. up on to a chair while the area is being cleaned. We feel that on the whole the ward is kept clean to a more than adequate standard. However, I do understand that from the point of view of the consumer this may not always appear to be the case. We would also like to explain that from time to time we may ask the domestic to leave certain patients' areas alone as the prospective upkeep of these areas is the responsibility of the patient as part of the care plan drawn up between nurse and patient.

I would like to thank you for drawing your concerns to my attention. I hope that you remain in good health.

Over the next few months you may be contacted by a member of staff from our Quality Development Department. These Quality Co-ordinators are undertaking a telephone audit survey, the results of which will be used by us to develop our procedures for handling complaints.

Should you remain dissatisfied with this response however, you have the right to request a review by the Trust Convenor within four weeks of the date of this letter.

Yours sincerely,

Acting Divisional General Manager

The day after I was admitted to the ward I noticed that the carpet in the room I shared sorely needed vacuuming. A couple of days later it had still not been cleaned and so I wrote a polite letter to the hospital manager reporting the situation. There was no reply and no change on the carpet cleaning front either. Other shortcomings in the ward environment had become apparent and so I wrote again, a bit short tempered this time:

> ...I wrote to you, the Acting Divisional General Manager, on Wednesday to report that the carpet in the room I share with four others had not been cleaned since the 20th [*of November, when I was admitted*]. It still, over a week later, has not been cleaned. I suspect that the floors of the admin offices are cleaned daily! I ask for two things: 1. The floor cleaned. 2. An explanation for this state of affairs.
>
> Besides the above I can report dirty, stained bed curtains, stained quilt covers, poorly kept toilets, furniture damaged leaving the impression of decay and neglect – this is not consistent with a therapeutic environment...

Another offence was the practice in that ward of patients drying their washing in the shared bedrooms due to broken down tumble-driers. Instead of having them repaired the hospital provided each room with a clotheshorse! Perhaps 'decay and neglect' was putting it a bit strong but something more significant than mere inattention to detail was going on.

A clue to the prime reason for the failure in cleanliness was the transformation which the weekend domestic worker brought about. By the end of that Saturday afternoon the floor was spotless and the toilet/shower room was sparkling. Conclusion: some hospital cleaners are much better at their jobs than others.

The cleaning supervisor, like the cleaners, was employed by a private contractor and so was not NHS staff. The overall responsibility for the ward environment lay with the Ward Manager. So patients shared a mucky room and toilet because a cleaner was not cleaning, a supervisor was not supervising and NHS management was not managing.

And, I am certain, because patients were not complaining. At the best of times as customers in restaurants etc., most of us find it difficult enough to complain; imagine how much more difficult and stressful complaining is as a patient in a psychiatric hospital. Here your spirits are as low as they can be; you want staff to care for you not see you as a threat.

After a couple of weeks of this particular hospital admission, too depressed for words, I quietly packed my bags and slipped out of the ward for the privacy of home. Later, though, in a more competent state I wrote to the hospital with more details and descriptions of the seediness I had encountered in that hospital room: patients' scattered, unwashed clothing and unmade beds; how some staff had found the untidiness amusing; the drying of washing in the rooms.

And so the opening rounds of a complaints marathon commenced. To begin with I only wanted them to acknowledge and attend to the shortcomings I had pointed out to them but that first letter (above) confronted me with an evil far greater than an unvacuumed ward floor. Things were to complicate awfully; I wanted blood!

Consider that statement in the second paragraph:

...We feel that on the whole the ward is kept clean to a more than adequate standard. However, I do understand that from the point of view of the consumer this may not always appear to be the case...

So, Mr and Mrs Psychiatric Patient, the carpet was actually vacuumed every day, it only *appeared* to be unvacuumed. The mucky carpet you lived with for a week was just a psychotic illusion – a symptom of your illness.

What point is there in psychiatric patients making complaints as long as there are senior NHS managers happy to explain a patient's complaint in terms of his illness?

After half a year of letters, meetings and an NHS enquiry I finally sent the inch-thick file to the Health Service Ombudsman; and although the Ombudsman's office rapped the Trust's knuckles for some of its procedural failings, it declined to investigate my complaints. Hard to accept and not much of a result for all the work I had put in.

As the thing got more and more difficult, I told myself that as I had the time and the ability to pursue the complaint I had a duty to do so on behalf of other patients and myself. This battle was something I could make myself useful with. But I am afraid I became obsessed with the issue. Here I was again: mounted on my white charger, fired with a rightful cause, to grips with a terrible enemy who, because I was right, I would certainly defeat. In that condition you would have had to drive over my head with a double-decker bus to close me up.

It has not yet sunk in that although I can look good for a while on that horse, sooner or later I am going to take a bullet and fall off it. The price I paid for that tangle with the NHS was a high one. Three years on I still flash back to the hiding I took. In depression it consumes me, along with the rest of the junk that musters in The Pits.

Eventually tumble-driers were supplied to the wards and fresh bed screens were brought in. This surprised me. All the managers should have done was look at the stained curtains long enough to see that they only *appeared* to need changing.

19

Concessionville – Getting Around

A community psychiatric nurse visited me for a while until I could not see the point of it any more. Maybe I would not have got into the pickle that got me hospitalized in 1997 if I had held on to her but there you are.

On her first visit she pointed out that being a manic-depressive I was entitled to a travel concession. The card worked first time and I have been flashing it around ever since on the north east's buses.

Twenty per cent off the full fare up to a maximum of two pounds is a great deal. Forty pence gets me the six miles to Fraserburgh and a quid gets me the forty miles to Aberdeen and, if I want to, onwards to any of the card's northern, western and southern limits of Nairn, Braemar or Montrose, not to mention places like Airyhall, Faulds Gate, Heatheryfold and other Aberdeen outplaces with strange sounding names; the card offers its holders the freedom of the big city too.

I had become a bus fan even before my card came along. Maybe it was just the power of positive thinking but the love affair began the day after I sold my last set of wheels. My motorbike was a rocket that made me eighteen every time I sat on it but it boiled down to a choice between the bills for the bike or the other things I needed to do. 'I can catch buses,' I told myself and so, with timetable in hand, I made a nervous start with a sortie into Aberdeen via a connection at Fraserburgh.

There are no bus stops around this country place; you just wave your bus down from wherever you are at the roadside. Along came my first country bus, from the Bluebird Bus Company (a Stagecoach outfit), the 270 Fraserburgh/New Pitsligo, a cheery Mercedes twenty-odd seater. Ten minutes later it breezed into Fraserburgh and with just two minutes to spare I transferred to my Aberdeen bus – another Bluebird job. So far so good I thought as I organized myself into my bit of upholstered space. The big city-bound Volvo was a much more accommodating prospect than its humble country cousin and as it pulled out of the bus station I sat back to enjoy the trip into Aberdeen.

And I did enjoy it. On that first coach ride into Aberdeen I realized how little I was going to miss personal transport. That journey and most of the others I have made since have been quality time; a part of life, not an unpleasant slice taken out of it. Now I ride through the Buchan countryside with *The Scotsman* and a Bounty chocolate bar, the road ahead somewhere up there in the hands of the uniformed driver, out of sight and out of mind.

This liberating gift from the council means that when combined with the arts concessions I am also entitled to, I can now get to and sit in the best seat of the house in the concert halls of Aberdeen sometimes for as little as a fiver. And I mean the 'best seat'; if the Queen were ever to attend a concert in the Aberdeen Music Hall it would be my seat she would get. Up here I lord it next to international names: pianists, cellists and violinists who have finished their solo performances and have come up to enjoy the rest of the night's programme; the latter's Strads practically dumped on my lap. The other concert-goers up here affect not to notice who has come amongst them but I always give the masters an approving smile as they join me; just a wee thing from me to top off the ovations they got from the crowd.

My difficulty with evening entertainment in the city is that there is no local bus service going past my track head after 7pm. This means that after my helping of city arts the last bus to Fraserburgh drops me off at midnight at the start of the black, four-mile, lonely walk home to my cottage.

But the distance depends a lot on what kind of night I have had; once, with my brain still full and fizzing with the Scottish National Jazz Orchestra, the walk only took a minute.

The real drawback is in winter when in preparation for the hike home I am forced to turn up at concerts as Sherpa Tensing. But then, on the other hand, when I had the motorbike, I used to go as Flash Gordon so perhaps no wheels is an improvement. I do it much less in winter these days though – it really has to be something special to get me polishing my hill walking boots for the opera.

There was a version of myself in which I used buses as therapy. It was a desperate measure which consisted of day-long journeys to anywhere. This was during my lithium/zombie period when just the going was needed, never mind where.

The road north was my favourite. Inverness can be done in a day but to get home the same day I must depart on the same bus fifteen minutes after its arrival – a helluva distance to go for a pee. Nairn was more feasible. Departing from the house at 6.30am I arrived for a pint and half an hour of its shops before catching the first of the next three buses (six in total) to get me home for 7.30pm. Full picnic gear was carried: newspapers, sunglasses, personal stereo and packed lunch with the highlight of the return journey being the opening of a bag of apple turnovers bought from Ashers Bakery Ltd, 150 High Street, Nairn. I look back and see how sad this stuff was, but I enjoyed the sleeps, was still usefully tired at night and survived again.

Bus drivers are like psychiatric nurses, some of them have nice personalities and some of them have not. As for their driving, I recall the particularly sunny driver of the last Fraserburgh bus out of Aberdeen waiting ten minutes outside the New Inn at Ellon to let a lassie run inside, we guessed, to attend to a pressing toilet need. That was perfect of him but the trouble was he put his bus into Ferrari mode until he had made up the time. These two incidents proving, I think, that there is no easy correlation to be made between friendliness and canniness.

My main tip for a long bus haul is never to cross your driver no matter how rude he or she has been. They might be as touchy or as depressed as you and you do not want them glowering at you in the passenger rear-view mirror all the way to Glasgow.

That community psychiatric nurse also told me about the organization Penumbra (I really should have held on to her). A penumbra can be described as the region at the boundary of an object. A bonny penumbra would be the soft halo or space around a backlit subject – not quite one thing or another, not quite solid, if you catch my drift.

Penumbra provides services for people with mental health problems and one of their respite residential places is in Aberdeen. There, in an elegant granite house in Aberdeen's posh West End, up to five guests are accommodated in comfort and privacy with as friendly a staff as you will find anywhere.

I have stayed there on a kind of holiday on two occasions since I became a full-time manic-depressive; having a time in the city which I could only have had by being independent and resident there and not having to pay a penny for my digs. Lounge about in the comfort of the house all you want but, by exploiting every concession going, I can afford to gorge on a packed week of shows, movies, plays, concerts and exhibitions without the distraction of thinking about that trek home at night.

During a time I was in hospital, lonely and in despair, I walked up to the house in search of a friendly face to speak to over a cup of coffee – which I found. This says everything about the staff at Penumbra and much about the staff that night in the ward.

From there I can also attend the monthly Aberdeen Manic Depression Fellowship meetings. On discovering that I had this midnight hike home after the meetings the Fellowship wrote to offer to pay for a taxi out of their funds.

What words are there for such a gesture from people who knew nothing about me other than that I was a manic-depressive? I could not accept; taking full and ruthless advantage of Concessionville is one thing, accepting kindness like that is another.

But back to buses. The National Federation of Bus Users offered bus passengers a first prize of £100 if the company they nominated won the 'Bus Company of the Year Award'. And so I wrote three pages in praise of Bluebird Buses. Okay, so with the hundred quid in my sights, I romanced a bit but it was fun to be so totally positive about something. A few months later the phone rang and I was being offered a trip to London for the presentation of the annual 'Welcome Aboard Awards'. My Bluebirds had not won but the Federation were so impressed by my three-page letter that they wanted to give me a special award – the then Transport Minister was to present it.

I was flown down. I was put with the minister for a photie and would have been flown home after the lunch if I had not opted to take the National Express overnight coach instead.

This gave me an afternoon and evening in London. My disability certificate (for my manic depression) got me into the museums at the disabled rate and the crutch (for my leg) had the bobbies in the Houses of Parliament opening doors and sending me up in an oak-lined lift to the Strangers' Gallery where I took in a couple of debates. Why the crutch? I happened to need one at the time due to a back and leg thing but it fitted the London script marvellously. I had laid out some personal stuff in my bid for the hundred quid: '…four-mile, lonely walk home to my cottage…when a long-standing illness meant I had to give up work…times when just pure going is needed, never mind where'. Nothing to hint that I was a 'psycho'. The crutch gave my London audience the physical cripple, which the occasion needed. The tinted glasses a friend offered me would, I think, have been overdoing it.

Does this make me not a nice person? Look, it avoided the strain of me knowing that the Transport Minister and the gathering of power-suited bus executives were wondering why such a cheerful and healthy-looking guy was: (a) unemployed, (b) pleading some kind of disability and (c) in their trough.

The crutch was a great success. One woman complimented me on my courage; another congratulated me on how I obviously enjoyed life to the full; the Transport Minister came down off the dais to give me my prize: 'What's the best way to do this?' I was asked.

I tell you I really needed that crutch to hold me up when my leg let me down every now and then. I did feel something of a fake, taking in all that admiration and consideration, but there was a tinge of anger too. My manic depression is a condition as disabling as anything I needed an aluminium stick for but if I had declared my psychosis, however cheerfully and carefully, never mind made explicit in some embarrassing moment of head-case behaviour, the conversations would have stopped very quickly. Would I even have been invited in the first place?

What the hell, I deserved this freebee. When I am in my best shape I grab at every chance going and every now and then one comes back with a grin on its face.

I enjoyed my afternoon and evening in London but the overnight bus home was a mistake. A cold, cramped, thirteen-hour pethidine-popping nightmare followed by spinal surgery a week later.

I was looking for a cheque but the heavy, gold wrapped package presented by the minister felt like a substantial book of some kind. I unwrapped it by the Thames. It was Issue 11 of *Bus Timetable Great Britain – 27th September to 15th February 1999*. My friend with the tinted glasses was delighted, said it served me right.

20

Show Folks – Social Wipeout

March 1997

Dear Brian,

The committee regrets that you were unwilling to meet with our representatives. We do not feel that it is appropriate that the whole committee meet with you on the terms intimated.

The committee wishes to express our dismay at and disapproval of your conduct towards our Chairperson and Vice-Chairperson.

Your physical and verbal abuse of committee members is deemed to be completely inappropriate and unacceptable in a family group such as ours and the committee reserves the right to terminate your membership should there ever again be verbal abuse towards or physical assault on any of our members.

We would also draw attention to the fact that all committee decisions on the management of the group are final.

We would stress that we offer you this opportunity to remain a member of the group only in the light of your previous involvement, which was, and still is, very much appreciated.

The committee is unanimous on this and we now consider the matter closed.

Yours sincerely,

[*Signatures of committee*]

There is no point in identifying the musical group or any individuals featured in this chapter. What matters are the events and the conclusions reached by the reader.

Brigadoon with a local musical society was my first musical as director. As described in Chapter Nine I was fired throughout the production of that show with a sustained and furious high but the cast were not to know that or of the terrible pressure I was under at work.

Although I was to direct for that musical society on another two occasions, I wanted to start something fresh in a local village. I found a woman who could sing a bit and she agreed to have a go at musical directing. She and her husband knew of folk in the surrounding area who would be interested in taking part and in no time a musical group was formed and a date fixed for its first show.

At the group's core were half a dozen middle-class families. All of them incomers to the area with few hailing from the north east of Scotland at all. It was clear that they had known one another for several years and that this adventure into amateur theatre was of social importance; something new for them to share as friends in their village experience, nothing wrong in that.

The first, modest show whetted everybody's appetites for more and in subsequent years I directed the next two shows, both of which I had written. My interest in amateur dramatics and playwrighting was given plenty of scope and, socially, my life had taken off as well. I was included at dinner parties, Christmas parties and Hogmanay parties and to the serial buffets and barbecues. Three years running I shared enjoyable holidays with some of the families. I enjoyed too the contact with children, all of whom were in my casts and with whom I worked in the youth theatre group I had also established in the village.

Although I did not shout it from the rooftops, I had made no secret of my manic depression and I am sure that through small gossip everybody would have come to know about it. The usual degree of ignorance and range of reactions to this would have been present but depressions and small highs came and went without there being anything disturbing for anyone to see. Rather, I felt trusted and valued and congratulated myself on falling in with such a friendly, generous bunch.

But as I became more dependent on them I also became more knowledgeable about them. The reality behind the various jollifications unravelled in tiny bits as some of the circle's members dripped out their little hatreds about one another: he was a fascist; she was worth watching; he was never at home; they were selfish; he was a misogynist; he used prostitutes; they were mean; what a boor he was; how stupid and artificial she was and how irresponsible he.

My analysis was that whilst there were some genuine friendships amongst them this was a group of colonists who had been around one another too long and who did not actually like one another very much. That, however, was unimportant; what was important was that they could trust one another not to show it. They could rub along perfectly well with people they disliked as long as the illusion of friendship was maintained and everybody had fun. The fun was real enough but beneath it a game of manners was being played out. A very serious game, for observing the rules and staying in the circle was part of surviving in a foreign land.

I also came to realize that this group was not naturally an inclusive one. Although the numbers of participants increased they were almost exclusively recruited from other families in the social circle or from friends of families already in it. This was not a group where someone coming off the street would have been made welcome but I never found anyone in the group capable of acknowledging this. A committee rule that only children who had parents involved in the productions could take part was another offence in the same vein.

In retrospect I look at all of this stuff and ask myself what was I doing amongst a completely self-serving clique but the truth was that the moments of uneasiness I felt were not long lasting. I felt that I had been fortunate: I had been befriended; I had something important in my life; with cast sizes of around forty adults and children and another thirty or so backstage it was highly rewarding to see so many people coming fresh into community theatre. With these people I had discovered my playwrighting ability, and they were happy to keep putting my work on the stage. Few writers had that going for them.

Then the world changed. Following the breakdown I described in Chapter Ten I had to pull out of directing the next show. My condition continued to deteriorate and eventually I was admitted to psychiatric hospital.

Two months later I came out of hospital and went home to a very lonely place indeed.

It was just before Christmas. Previous festive seasons in the village had been great fun but not this one: no visitors, no invitations to anybody's home or to that year's New Year's Eve party, no phone calls, nothing. Perhaps I could have taken some initiative but I retreated into a world I knew fine from before. Two people, valued friends to this day, were to emerge out of these depths but that year I watched Christmas and New Year's Eve on TV.

Three months later I worked uneasily backstage on that year's show *The King and I*. Not having been involved in the rehearsals this was the first I had seen of some of the group for many months. Everybody seemed pleased to see me but, although I did have some friends there, I knew what I was dealing with now. Most of the smiles from the folk in that hall meant very little and neither, of course, did mine. Was this me now playing the game of manners myself and playing it as desperately as anyone ever had? Most of my social life and my challenges were here. At that time it seemed that there was nowhere else for me to go.

In May I went off to the hills for five days and when I came back I found a letter notifying me that the group's AGM had taken place the previous day. I was annoyed and hurt by the carelessness that had caused me to receive such late notice as, keen to get back into the swing of things, I had wanted to join the committee.

My request to be co-opted on to the committee was turned down. When they picked a show they could not possibly produce, *Chicago*, I tried to tell them but was scoffed at. Clearly I was not an alpha male any more. (Their musical director came along later and made them dump it.)

A summer and autumn passed without seeing much of anybody and I spent another New Year on my own. I was to do the lighting in the next show but only after pushing my way into the job. It would have been far better if I had stayed away. An issue over safety arose in which the access gangway to an auditorium fire escape was to be obstructed by an oversized stage extension and an improvised and wholly unsafe alternative escape created elsewhere.

When amateurs start improvising in theatres hand out the safety helmets! My concerns, which I put forward several times over a week, were boorishly rejected by the stage manager and only after a public argument I had with his wife was the fire escape reinstated. She says I verbally abused her. It was actually a row – easy to get the two confused if you want to.

They widened the gangway.

It was not a pleasant show week but the sequel to the argument over safety was catastrophic. During the clearing up after the show an attempt was made by one of the committee to remove from me an extensive collection of lighting filters and other lighting bits and pieces which I had accumulated and cared for in over twenty-five years of participation in community theatre. Petty stuff but it was revenge time.

This man had been in the background until now but here he was out in the street with the mob. He had been a particular friend and although, like the rest, I had seen much less of him and his family in recent times he was somebody I still trusted. It took a moment for the seriousness of what he was doing to sink in.

The confrontation appeared to have been planned. It was too much. My temper went and in the face of my protests (and, I fear, the obscenities) he backed off but only to return a moment later with the stage manager who, literally, had been lurking in the wings – the attempted dispossession had been planned all right.

Another altercation took place and it went to bits when I punched my former friend – an impotent, helpless jab at his chest (I couldn't hit anybody for peanuts). He could have me for assault, he called out for the dozen or so others in the hall, and my stomach twists again as I flashback to his playground level taunt: 'But we know you're having your problems.'

Okay, he was in a state by this time too, but here my 'problems', my psychiatric illness, was being thrown at me in the village hall by a grown man, a man who had been my friend.

So he and others had noticed that I was having 'problems'. This was why they had welcomed me back with open arms after my two months in hospital and why he and his fellow bully had attempted to strip me of the lighting equipment after having stripped me of everything else.

At the time I was desperately ashamed and embarrassed at having struck him but later I came to dwell more on how fine it would have been if I could have given him the smack he deserved. A movie thump with full sound effects, the kind that sends the bad guy sliding ten yards backwards on his backside across the floor.

The committee, in full corporate bully mode, wrote me their letter and after a waste of letters from me to them and a final look at their faces at the next AGM, that was the last I saw of any of them. I learned a few weeks later that it was common knowledge in the village that I had attempted to sabotage the show. That's show biz!

What, looking back on the affair as dispassionately as I can, do I make of it all now? Why this treatment from a group of people who should have felt nothing but gratitude to me for the life-enhancing avenue I had led them along?

Of course I cannot be sure about all the factors and the dynamics involved, but what I believe basically happened was that individuals becoming more competent wanted more power in the running of the shows and my time out of the scene was their chance to blossom. I then broke the rule that required that the illusion of friendship be maintained and that the fun must not be spoiled. What I was expected to do with my new low status was accept it with a smile, certainly not try to push my way on to the committee and embarrass the troupe's high ranking members by exposing important safety failings and other poor decisions.

But what I am certain of is the impact my illness, post-psychiatric hospital, had upon how I was viewed and how I was treated. My manic depression was now no longer a thing that people had just heard about or puzzled or gossiped about. My mental illness was now a thing with repulsive detail in it. I had taken a knife to my arms and my face; I had been on the roof when the doctor came; I had been in a mental hospital for two months.

This group would have been no different to any other group in society in containing a high proportion of people (perhaps a majority) who will always be uncomfortable around psychiatric illness. With my elevation to basket-case, some would have found it difficult to have me close. But here also I am sure I detected individuals prepared, not just to exploit my absence, but to use my illness against me. In this kind of process someone with a psychiatric illness or a history of psychiatric illness may not just be enthusiastic or disappointed or inspired or angry or determined any more: all emotional behaviour is seen as irrational and symptomatic of their illness – especially if they need to be kept in their place or discredited.

My manic depression did have a lot to do with my behaviour that week but that did not mean to say that everything I thought and did was invalid. I became obsessed with that fire escape; certain that I was right and everybody else was wrong, it was a cause that I could not let go of no matter what the consequences for me were. This also was a time when I was first experiencing the fragile state that has remained to some extent with me to this day. I am very easily knocked off balance, suffering greatly from any slight or injustice. Here the knocks came aplenty and my mind was in constant turmoil. Yes, I was not very well, these folk helped with that, but I was never mad and never bad.

Here's the difference between a response to psychiatric disability and a response to a physical one: if I had returned from two months in a general hospital paralysed in a shiny wheelchair for the rest of my life, I would have had to fight off the kindnesses – ways would have been cleared, ramps would have been installed, toilets would have been fitted out. I would have needed a sack to carry my 'Get Well Soon' cards home. Every allowance would have been made, it being a privilege to join with me in my courageous battle back to my previous life. Nobody would have dared try to do me down.

'What's the next show going to be then, Brian? We need you, you know.'

21

The Choir Lady – Making Things Worse

Visit a ward in any general hospital and you will see that most of the beds are festooned with flowers and 'Get Well Soon' cards. In a psychiatric ward the norm is just a few cards or none at all. The choir lady in this recent story gave away one of the reasons, one that had never occurred to me: the psychiatric in-patient is not properly ill.

A couple of years on from the village musical scene disaster I joined a choir in another part of Aberdeenshire and had a few enjoyable sings with them but just before the next session's rehearsals started, I was back in a psychiatric hospital with a depression.

From the ward I phoned up a choir member and told her that I could not manage to attend the rehearsals. I was in hospital, I told her, with this 'ongoing thing'; deliberately suggesting that it was my spine that had put me in hospital (I was still moving about with a crutch after the last operation on my back).

But I had miscalculated. 'What ward are you in?' the lady wanted to know. The choir members would all want to send me cards. 'No, no, that's all right,' I said. 'But we like to send cards,' she insisted. 'What ward are you in? C'mon, Brian.'

'Ward 40,' I lied. This was the ward where I had had a second operation on my back half a year ago. Feeling displeased with myself and surprised at the loss of confidence I had shown, I spoke to the Ward Manager and asked if he would assist me in my deceit by phoning Ward 40 and ask them to forward to his ward any mail addressed to me.

Up smiled the Deputy Ward Manager, who had been listening: 'And what if a couple of choir ladies show up at Ward 40 with a bunch of flowers asking for Brian Adams?'

Mmnnn....

I phoned the choir lady right away and apologized for misleading her. I told her that I was in a psychiatric hospital with manic depression. Sorry for thinking that she would be embarrassed by it, I did not mind her telling anybody she wanted to that I was in hospital with this illness and that cards should be sent to this ward in the psychiatric hospital.

She could not have been nicer about it and I realized what a dope I had been in trying to conceal the truth and how much worse I had made things. Despite my willingness for anybody to know of my situation, she said she would be careful whom she told and that she was very glad that I had told her about my manic depression because when she had put the phone down after speaking to me earlier that day, she was terribly concerned that there was something 'really seriously' wrong with me.

Mmnnn....

Two cards from choir members came in the following day which I appreciated and which doubled my total in one swoop.

22

Only a Salt – Prescription Drugs

In *Dr Mike Smith's Handbook of Prescription Medicines* he quotes a survey carried out in the late 1980s which revealed that more than half of patients questioned did not know when or with what they should take their medicines and that about eight in ten had not been warned about potential side effects.

Some doctors, I think, prefer their patients to be in this state of ignorance. A junior doctor on a psychiatric team once said to me that if she told patients what side effects to watch out for they would just go and get them.

Okay, I think we can see something in that. It's just that I, for one, have always managed to get my side effects without being told in advance. Presumably that doctor would find my reporting of impotence and hair loss to be all the more credible for my being in ignorance of these as a drug's potential side effects, whereas the patient presenting these horrors after being warned about them can somehow be accused of inflicting balding and not getting it up upon himself!

Okay, we know how suggestible we all are but it is best to know what is going on in your body, I think. It once took several weeks for the penny to drop that it was the side effect of an anti-depressant that was causing my manhood difficulties and not some new and terrible psychological challenge to add to my manic depression experience.

There is, in fact, plenty of information available about prescription drugs. Everything from 99p drug guides to the material published by the multitude of sufferers' organizations. In the case of we manic-depressives this includes a comprehensive collection of books, booklets, leaflets, research papers, summaries, newsletters, magazine articles etc. and, of course, there is the mass of stuff available on the internet. When that doctor finds out she's going to be very annoyed!

Lithium carbonate is the drug I have most experience of. It has helped many people and it may have helped me too, but my reading of its associated literature encouraged me to have my blood scrupulously monitored and to pay close attention to my body's goings-on. This, for someone of my hypochondriacal tendencies, was great fun but it did seem like the sensible thing to do. Too little lithium and you are wasting your time, too much and the stuff will make you ill.

It has to be said, though, that the experts have the capacity to confuse. One information sheet I have is disarmingly relaxed about the drug and only describes a few 'minor' nuisances to put up with: gastrointestinal disturbances, tremor, weight gain, thirst, increased urination. Another laid back publication placed kidney damage and thyroid changes in only the 'intermediate side effects' category!

The following are drawn from various books and publications:

Question 1 How long does it take for lithium to take effect?

Answer A   'It can take anything from a few days to several weeks for any noticeable improvement to take place.'

Answer B   'Sometimes it is several months before the full preventative effect is in evidence.'

Answer C   'It may take up to a year to exercise its full effect.'

Answer D   'Another fast-acting drug used in the treatment of bipolar depression is lithium carbonate.'

Question 2 Are there any problems in coming off lithium?

Answer A   'There is no withdrawal syndrome on cessation of use.'

Answer B   'Never stop taking lithium abruptly.'

Answer C   'It should be withdrawn gradually, preferably under medical supervision.'

Then there was the TV phone-in psychiatrist telling Susan from Suffolk to relax about her lithium:

TV Psychiatrist

It is actually just a salt. But if you can, just think of it as a salt, a kind of table salt. We all have table salt every day. There's no reason why you couldn't just see yourself as just having a salt deficiency which needs to be topped up by the lithium.

Harry Ramsden

Anything on it, Madam: red sauce, black sauce, vinegar, table salt, sea salt, lithium carbonate?

After two years on lithium I was sure that, apart from the niggling nuisances of thirst and itching, the drug was disagreeing with me. Episodes of devastating fatigue and a stifling flatness seemed to point to lithium as the culprit. And so another tack was tried: depot injections (long-lasting) of flupenthixol, an anti-psychotic medication. Within twenty-four hours I was crazed with the stuff and the encounter led to a stay in hospital.

After the crisis was over I could have taken something to counteract the side effects and given the stuff another go but not bloody likely. To understand you would have had to have been where I had been. Through good luck and an immediate conference between GP and psychiatrist, the former was at my door with something to put an end to it.

This 'good luck' was the abusive letters I had sent to them both. Little notes to tell them how useless they were. I thought that I was going to be in hell forever. Out of my mind, it never occurred to me to get down to the surgery and ask politely for help. But it could have been a lot worse – if I had known the side effects beforehand it could have been really nasty.

Doctor [*Withdrawing hypodermic needle from patient's backside.*] Right this injection will do you for a month. Now, in the short-term, the drug may result in pseudo parkinsonism, insomnia, impotence, extreme anxiety and restlessness, putting your shirt on back to front and sending me hate mail. Long-term, we are looking at Tardive Dyskinesia which you are in with at least a twenty-five per cent chance of developing – damage to your central nervous system causing uncontrollable blinking and tongue movements, twitching of the lips and face, twisting of the hands, tapping of the feet, crossing and uncrossing of the legs, shrugging of the shoulders, uncontrollable rocking and possibly breathing difficulties.

Reversal of the drug's side effects can take years and may not be complete but I'm pretty sure that it will make you feel a lot better.

'Doctor knows best,' a voice says; you have to trust your doctors.

And yes you (more or less) should. I have (more or less) trusted every doctor I have ever had and, in the most part, it has paid off. The qualification mainly refers to the one who diagnosed a punctured lung instead of the heart infection I had and left me to suffocate at four in the morning. But one cock-up is not bad for a fifty-three year surgery and hospital ward trail to here via the dozen places I have lived.

But it is not simply a question of trusting my doctors. What makes me nervous about taking long-term drugs is not so much the risks and the side effects of the stuff but the requirement for me and everybody in the NHS system I am in, to manage my drug therapy correctly, all of the time, for the rest of my life.

The following incidents happened to me over a two-year period: drug monitoring failing due to my blood being put into the wrong bottle and then not being recalled for more blood to enable the test to be redone; a pharmacist sending me home with a bottle of tranquillizers instead of anti-depressants (chlorpromazine instead of clomipramine); a hospital nurse making exactly the same mix-up (only I swallowed hers); late monitoring of a fever I had as a psychiatric in-patient whilst on lithium. There is also the potential harm I can do to myself by making mistakes and twice I have made serious ones.

So there have been times when I have wondered if in my head-case, are the risks and unwanted effects of long-term medication not worse than the illness itself?

If the side effects of aspirin included hot flushes and impotence, like a tranquillizer I once had a hoot with, somehow I feel that most people would be happy to wait for their headaches to pass. And the risks women take with the contraceptive pill seem tiny compared to the risks of some of the stuff which people like me are presented with; I see nothing of the public scrutiny that the pill gets.

I wonder if there are people out there taking drugs long-term just to be more acceptable to society: to be kept quiet, kept out of sight, to keep a salary coming in, to spare ferry queues from clowning backpackers. I, long since, got fed up of showing off to ferry queues and the like and am grateful at this time for a medication that keeps me quietly in the queue rather than showing off outside of it. But if people want to juggle or sing in the street or even be a bit of a nuisance, it surely does not justify giving them a drug to shut them up.

The spoiler with lithium in the past has been its flattening effect. The drug may have given me the summer in which I took off on a series of week-long solo treks in the mountains of Scotland but only, I thought at the time, by driving me out of my house in a desperate bid to distract me from its imprisonment.

Things did ease and the summer turned out to be a memorable one. But which do I thank most for the memories – the unpleasant effects of the drug for chasing me into the hills or its therapeutic qualities for making it possible? My thanks to whichever but in future I fancy that I will not be panicked into early April backpacking treks in the Cairngorms – that first outing could have got me killed a couple of times over.

In September of that year, now well soused in lithium, the flatness completely took over and with it the crippling fatigue that was to dog me for the next fifteen months. The world became a spiritless, unseasoned place in which I became detached from everything; mentally shuffling about in a place in which I could tell what a funny joke or a beautiful painting was all right but somehow could not quite register them emotionally. Imagine sinking your teeth into your favourite food but not tasting it; that was my experience of life with lithium. In my second year of this I often mistook this condition for depression. Depression is depression whatever its causes but this had a different quality to it.

My social isolation had increased and the room-wandering despair I experienced along with this flatness was, I now realize, chronic loneliness. This was a completely new experience for me. I have lived on my own for most of my life and have come to value it. Solitude suits me as long as I have purpose but, lithium-saturated, daytime television and aimless trips on buses were as purposeful as I could get.

For lithium watchers, the drug did not prevent an episode of mania. On my mania scale of one to ten it started as a mere 'three'. A 'three' is good – no rooftops or Stanley knives. Just clarity, the world looking good, feeling great (not as in 'Napoleon-great' that is) and, in this particular episode, the bit of harmless showing off to the queue on Craignure Pier.

And so, what with the continuation of this zombie state and persistent fatigue, I stopped taking lithium. Enter flupenthixol, the consensus being that I did better on 'something'. But that glimpse of the abyss made me forget and forgive lithium everything and so, after a chat in the hospital ward headed 'Where Do We Go From Here', at my own suggestion I was back on it.

But before it kicked in there was a wonderful fatigue-free period and the high that got me started on this book. Then that old lithium feeling took over and everything died again.

The situation seemed clear to me: lithium was poisoning me. On the positive side of it there had been no severe depressions and only one minor hypomanic episode in twenty months spoke for itself. Fine, all of that, but the trouble was that for most of time there was nobody at home.

I have started taking lithium again and confusingly, ten months on, there have not been any suggestion of side effects. Do not let my unhappiness with lithium suggest that I have it down as dangerous junk. You want the stuff to work; for some sufferers lithium carbonate has changed their life.

The late Spike Milligan, whose manic depression was well documented, suggested on camera that lithium was helping him. He looked good on BBC Two's *Spike Night*, an event held to celebrate his eightieth birthday. I wept once to see him powerless in a depression and I was ready to switch the television off at the first sign of him in another. But he was good enough for me. He delivered an appallingly rude joke and with the next question linked it to an answer that soared above the banality offered:

Interviewer   What advice would you give to young comics, Spike?

Milligan   Keep it clean.

I hope that Spike was a successful lithium responder and I wonder as he took some potentially talent-inhibiting drug whether he feared the loss of the verseless, Goonless, Puckoonless version of himself in return for a life free from his terrible depressions?

When he spoke about these depressions the atmosphere changed. Sorry, but only folk like him and me know what he was talking about.

Manic depression propaganda claims that it would be a dull world without the 'genius disease'. If Spike's illness was part of his genius, the price he paid for brightening the world has been an appalling one.

23

Another Way of Being – Something to Celebrate?

All I remember about writing this final chapter was how great it felt. Now, a few weeks later, struggling to get this book finished as a depression sets in, I am no longer the same man who started this chapter, soaring in the fine form that follows.

With this book I have been on a journey in which I have had my say and my fun but it has been a journey in which I have thought about my situation more deeply than ever before. The question I have arrived at is who or what am I with this illness now that I appear to be stuck with it? Incidentally, only at a point in writing this book did it strike home that I *was* stuck with it. I have been a manic-depressive for over twenty-five years, been diagnosed for thirteen but it has taken this review of my life with it for its permanency to truly sink in.

Maybe an illness which influences my personality so powerfully, a thing that operates at the very core of me, is part of me to the extent that it actually is me and that to talk exclusively in terms of suffering from it is to miss out on some of the truth.

There is certainly suffering involved, but it is a suffering which arises out of being a particular, valid, important form of life rather than arising from some pointless disease. Valid and important because I'm not having anyone telling me that my life has been for nothing just because it has been so chaotic and interrupted. I know what I have contributed along the way and I know the good things I have collected too.

But I do not view myself as a man-overcoming-huge-personal-challenge-turning-it-into-a-positive-force-kind-of-hero. The opposite is more the case: I am certain that every useful thing I have produced has been enabled by the power my illness has given me; I achieved this and that because of my manic depression not in spite of it.

I am manic depression and manic depression is me; if there is a manic-depressive gene, I carry that gene and that gene carries me; I am that mental illness which medicine describes as Manic-Depressive Psychosis or Bipolar Mood Disorder. I am also a complexity of other things, some of which I can possibly take the credit for, but at my core, dominating everything through the sheer force of its/my personalities, is the manic-depressive illness. Is that not the plain or, depending on how adventurous (or manic) I want to be, the exciting truth?

But at this stage of the game I have had enough excitement, thank you, just the truth about this illness will do.

First, an 'illness' is, I am sure, what this is. As uncomplimentary and negative as the word might seem for a condition so unique in its creative potential, it is, nevertheless, the right word. A strange kind of illness, for sure, but I do not think that you would want to experience the level of elation and obsession which I experience now as I write, or want to have been inside van Gogh's head when he painted the *Wheatfield.* What else can mania be but an illness when you are out of control and bankrupting yourself again with unfettered generosity and crazy financial schemes? What else can depression be but a cripplingly ill-met thing? Suicidal obsession cannot be anything other than a potentially terminal illness.

But to cope with the idea of being a walking, talking, thinking, singing, beautiful lump of pathology I need to look for a more positive, helpful and creative view of my situation. I need to do a little work on the word 'illness'.

I recall a television medic/philosopher speaking about all illnesses as 'another way of being'. Whilst I doubt if your average kidney stone patient would be able to embrace his agony in any kind of philosophical way at all it is, nevertheless, a view of illness which helps me to explore what I am.

It would be easy to take off with that idea and develop a case for a new, celebratory notion of manic depression, something much more positive than is suggested in the unglamorous labels: 'illness', 'sick', 'sufferer'. I'd love to lead us all into an upper, positive, elitist plane and proclaim a higher, non-medical status for our uniqueness.

I buy some of it. This *is* a different way of being, one that can be special and useful; but the sobering reality is that it is to medicine I always run when the going gets too hard. In the depths of my next depression I will go knocking at the surgery door looking for therapies and protection from a doctor; not, I think, go looking for good ideas from philosophers and people like me on good form.

So my 'Another Way Of Being' slogan is unlikely to find its way on to my T-shirt but, armed with this cheerful thought, maybe I can embrace my illness a bit more; no longer embarrassed by it, no longer apologizing for it; happy, if need be, to define myself as a manic-depressive and let that be all the explanation that anybody is going to get.

What have I to lose? My bridges are all burned; I have no job to risk, no money to squander, no Rotary nomination to blow. As long as the state is prepared to help out and I can sell the odd feature and win the odd writing prize to pay for luxuries like new specs, I will not have to beg in the streets.

Hardest is learning how to take one day at a time but I think I have it now. Not in a year of AGMs do you find me chairing it in committee, bossing it in rehearsal rooms or wanting to influence the mob, combo, party, movement, mole hunt, team, crow shoot troupe or anything that will kick me when I am down. The project is the solo and selfish one of the fulfilment and protection of me and if it is not inconsistent with the above, the holding on to of my friends.

I mourn the loss of the world in which for most of the time I used to be able to mix it but drugs, in the end, have failed to keep me there. Sure, it was to take away the pain that I took the carbamazepine, the sodium valproate, the flupenthixol, the lithium carbonate, the fluoxetine, the methotrimeprazine, the diclophenac sodium and all the other stuff I have forgotten about. The prime objective, however, was to stay in the game, to be a player in it and, yes, to be acceptable to the crowd as unforgiving, fickle, hypocritical and stigmatizing as, from here, I can see it is. My friends definitely got better when they got fewer.

At this time I have swung up to a happy and productive period. All engagements with my friends are a stream of joy and good humour and being a stranger is no protection from me. I was far too gabby on the bus into town yesterday but the woman and her two young children seemed happy with my patter. The worst she would have thought was that I was perhaps just a bit eccentric – a character. On the other hand maybe she just saw a friendly guy who teased the kids with his magic tricks.

This is mild hypomania, easygoing stuff, but I feel it darkening into something else, something uncomfortable. The writing of this book is beginning to dominate everything again, it is no longer the pure pleasure it was a week ago. I have been here many times before, of course: twenty-four-hour writing days, the discomfort, the loss of the rest of my life.

It will pass in a week or so and I might get a settled summer but, then, when did I last have a completely settled summer? Yesterday on the bus I was a magician; tomorrow depression might hit me and Elvis, the ticket inspector, could board at the Post Office and lead the passengers in *Blue Suede Shoes* and all I would do is notice how dirty the bus windows were. Then I would be that moody bloke who sometimes speaks to you and sometimes doesn't. None of that is troubling anyone too much and, well, too bad if it does.

That hypomanic attack is long past. Now, half a year later, depression prevails and only a few words are possible. Maybe there is something of value in this final chapter but I look at the brave words of the version of me that wrote them – how reckless and ridiculous most of it is – and wonder who he was. I am to have ECT again.